ART & DISABILITIES : ESTABLISH
NX 180 H34L84 1990

DATE DUE

~~JAN 7 '94~~			
~~APR 5 '99~~			
~~NO 16 '05~~			

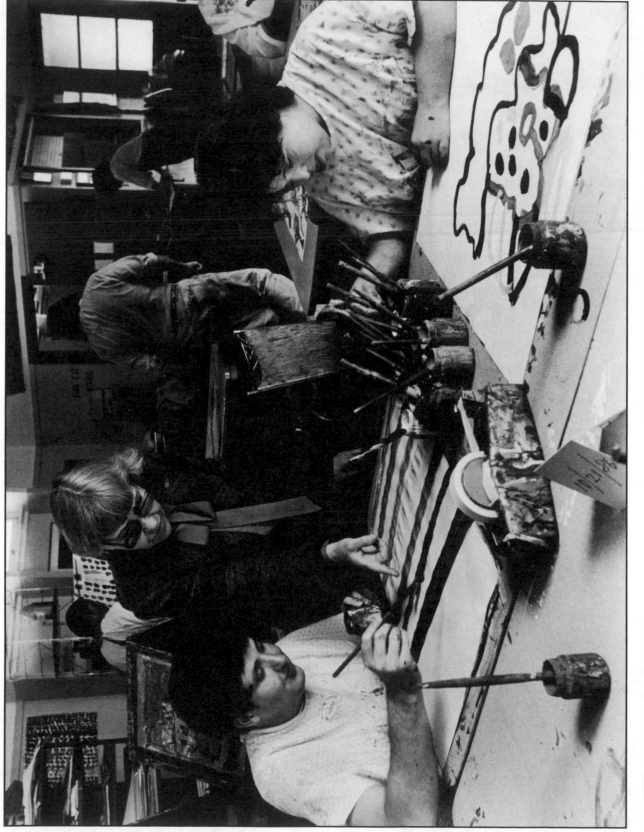

ART

& Disabilities

Establishing the Creative Art Center for People with Disabilities

by Florence Ludins-Katz, MA. and Elias Katz, Ph.D.

BROOKLINE
BOOKS

Library of Congress Cataloging-in-Publication Data

Ludins-Katz, Florence
    Art & disabilities: establishing the creative the creative art center for people with disabilities/Florence Ludins-Katz and Elias Katz.
      p.   cm.
    Includes bibliographical references.
    ISBN 0-914797-51-4 : $24.95
    1. Handicapped and the arts--United States. 2. National Institute of Art and Disabilites. I. Katz, Elias, 1912- . II. Title.
III. Title: Art and disabilities.
NX180.H34L84 1990.
707'.1'5--dc20   89-23983
                                        CIP

Printed by
Brookline Books

OTHER BOOKS. . .

By Florence Ludins-Katz and Elias Katz
 Creative Art of the Developmentally Disabled
 Art & Disabilities (First Edition)
 Freedom to Create
 The Creative Spirit

By Elias Katz
 Childrens Preferences for Traditional and Modern Paintings
 The Retarded Adult in the Community
 The Retarded Adult at Home
 Mental Health Services for the Mentally Retarded

ABOUT THE AUTHORS. . .

Florence Ludins-Katz, M.A. (Columbia University)
Exhibiting artist, art teacher, art critic, lecturer, author, administrator

Elias Katz, Ph.D. (Columbia Univeristy)
Clinical psychologist, lecturer, author, administrator

They are at present Co-Directors of the National Institute of Art and Disabilites, a nonprofit, tax-exempt corporation which operates an art program for adults with disabilties and art classes for disabled children. The Institute exhibits the art of people with disabilites, offers professional training, conducts workshops, conferences and lectures, publishes books and produces videotapes in the field of art and disabilties.

Acknowledgments

This books is dedicated to the many people who in spite of disabilites have created a unique and powerful art.

We wish to thank our many colleagues and friends with whom we have been associated for many years, especially Pearl Rand, for their encouragement and involved.

We are grateful to foundations, corporations and individuals, as well as federal, state, country and city agencies.

All of these have believed in the ideas expressed in this book and have supported the art center for people with disabilites.

We express deep appreciation to the four art centers for people with disabilites which we founded during the past fifteen years, for the experience we gained and the pleasure we have had in working with them:

National Institute of Art and Disabilities, Richmond
Creative Growth, Oakland
Creativity Explored, San Francisco
Creativity Unlimited, San Jose

We wish to acknowledge the many individuals throughout the United States and Canada who have accepted the philosophy put forth in this book and have dedicated themselves to promoting the art of people with disabilites.

Preface

At present there is a tremendous need for creative Art Centers for people with disabilities. Whenever we meet with those who work with disabled persons we find excitement and enthusiasm about the idea of developing the creative artistic potentials which lie dormant in disabled persons. Parents, artists and art teachers, educators, mental health professionals, social agencies, disabled persons, and the general public have expressed intense interest in establishing Art Centers which will bring out the creativity of disabled people.

In contrast to earlier beliefs, there is widespread agreement that disabled people not only belong in the community but should be active members of the community, and should not be forced to exist in state institutions isolated from their fellow-citizens. As a consequence, large numbers of disabled persons now live in the community. But the question remains—how can they lead more normal lives? Certainly it is not normal to wander about the streets or to remain isolated in one's room at home. Therefore it becomes necessary to provide many different types of community activities and facilities to meet their special needs and desires.

There are many organizations and individuals striving to establish Art Centers for persons with disabilities in their communities. Many of these will be successful in the near future. Some have become bogged down or have given up because they have started without realizing the dimensions of the task, the ground work, and the steps which must be taken in order to make the Art Center in the community an actuality.

In addition to free standing Art Centers we believe that creative art classes should be an integral part of mental hospitals, jails, convalescent hospitals, boarding homes for disabled persons, residential schools for handicapped persons, etc. Art programs add to the enrichment of life for those confined to these settings and enrich the environment in the whole institution. The principles and suggestions in this book are applicable to all art programs and art classes in both residential and day programs for disabled persons. To be more specific, a chapter is included on how to establish art classes within the framework of an existing organization, institution or school.

However, the main part of the book is devoted to the establishment of an Art Center which has many similarities to an art studio or an art school. Disabled persons come of their own volition. They work as artists and regard themselves as art students or as artists. They have an opportunity to exhibit their work and share it with others and in turn the community is enriched by their strength and creative power.

Since we have gone through the process of setting up several visual Art Centers for disabled persons, we know this can be accomplished. We find a certain commonality in the problems faced and the solutions found. We are including philosophy, need for community support, fund raising approaches, job descriptions, budgets, volunteer activities, studio setups, adaptations of equipment, art experiences, etc., to make the job of establishing such a Center less difficult.

This book is not meant to be the solution to all problems but is intended to be a practical resource. It will be used differently by different people in different communities. It is an effort to answer the numerous requests for guidance we have received. We hope that the establishment of the National Institute of Art and Disabilities will be of great help in answering serious questions that constantly arise in this field.

But beyond and above the practical information we wish to stimulate the forces of creativity both in establishing these Centers as well as in developing the students as artists. It is our hope that all who use this book will benefit in some way.

Florence Ludins-Katz, M.A.
Elias Katz, Ph.D.
Berkeley, California
1990

(Throughout this book we have consistently used the masculine gender only because we have not found a better term. In all instances we make no distinction between the feminine and the masculine.)

The Artist Speaks

When I am in my painting I am not aware of what I am doing. It is only after a sort of "get acquainted" period that I see what I have been about. I have no fears about making changes, destroying the image, etc., because the painting has a life of its own. I try to let it come through. It is only when I lose contact with the painting that the result is a mess. Otherwise there is pure harmony, an easy give and take, and the painting comes out well.

Jackson Pollock
Man & His Symbols
Edited with an Introduction
by C.G. Jung
Dell Publishing, 1964, p. 308

I believe in the magic and the miracles of the art experience. The creative process of direct encounter with a work of art is one of the most pure educational processes there is.

Communications with another human being through a visual expression can be extraordinarily powerful. There's no way you can experience a work of art, walk outside, and not experience the world differently. That's what art does. It has that special ability to sneak up behind your head, alter perceptions, help you relate to the world you live in.

I'm a religious fanatic when it comes to art and what it can do. Nothing else has that incredible power to subconsciously attack your mind. To make art is the most revolutionary act. The liberty that art gives one is extraordinary.

George Neubert
Focus, June 1982, Vol. 29, #6
Formerly Associate Director of Art,
San Francisco Museum of Modern Art

Table of Contents

I.
Philosophy

Chapters 1-4

1 Creativity

Why is it so necessary to foster creativity in all people? Do severely handicapped persons have lesser needs for expression or is their expression of less importance?

Our philosophy is that each person has the right to the richest and fullest development of which he is capable. Only then can society reach its fullest potential. Since we believe that creativity is the highest actualization of human functioning, it is of paramount importance to provide an environment in which creativity is appreciated, stimulated, and encouraged.

Creativity is a vital living force that lies within each individual. It may be repressed, unused. At times it may seem to fade away but it never dies. It enables man to transcend himself and his environment.

Creativity is the core of man. It urges him to do things that are satisfying to him. He may polish a stone just for the feel of it—or he may put nicks into it to satisfy his sense of touch—or he may place a drop of color on it for the pleasure it brings him—and then, he may give it to someone so that he can share his joy and his sense of accomplishment. Just a little thing—just a pebble picked up on the shore—but man's creativity transforms it and somehow, in this act, he has also transformed himself and his environment.

Defining Creativity

We find it necessary to try to define creativity so that we can better communicate our feelings and thoughts. It is like trying to pin down a cloud or a breeze. So much eludes definition; so much is lost.

Creative self-expression is the outward manifestation in an art form of what one feels internally. This expression may find its outlet in painting, sculpture, music, dance, poetry or in many other forms. It may be inspired by what one sees or experiences in the environment or a transformation of it; or, it may be a reaction to inner moods, feelings, or sensations.

The essence of this definition is that creativity lies within the individual and must be expressed for well-being and growth. Although there is a terrific drive for sharing, it is not necessarily a part of the creative act.

Let us pull this definition apart to see whether it has real meaning in explaining what we are trying to communicate.

"Creative self-expression is the outward manifestation in an art form of what one feels internally." By this we mean the complete involvement of the person in expressing his feelings. He may not be aware of exactly how he feels. But the sensation still exists—sometimes very low-key, sometimes explosive—for which he must find an outlet. Given the right environment, we feel that this force will result in a creative act. This is not limited to the savage or the sophisticate, to the genius or to the retarded, to one civilization or to another. We find creativity in aboriginal artists, in prehistoric artists, in renaissance artists, and in twentieth century artists. It cannot be produced for money or for external rewards. It is like breathing: for the organism to live, it must be there.

Can creative self-expression be an internal feeling with no outward manifestation? Internal feelings are an essential part of all of us, but these feelings in themselves are not creative self-expression. How many times do we paint a wondrous picture in our mind or sing a song within our brain? Not until that picture goes on a canvas or a wall, not until that song is translated into music or words, is there real creativity. This is the difference between dream and reality, and creative self-expression is a reality.

It may be inspired by what one sees or experiences in the environment or a transformation of it. So often a person walks through the city streets, looks up at the tall buildings, feels himself so small, so insignificant, and then suddenly it dawns upon him that without him and people like him there would be nothing there. He gets a feeling in his gut. He wants to share with others, to portray his feelings, to make his feelings known. Perhaps tonight he will go to his studio and he will paint. But what he paints may not be tall buildings but a feeling of infinity in which he and the buildings are merged.

A person walks through a forest. When he comes home he may paint the forest, or he may paint one tremendous tree trunk that symbolizes for him the eternal meaning of "tree" or "life."

It may be a reaction to inner moods, feelings, or sensations. So often we ourselves are not aware of what stimulates us, of what changes our moods or feelings. We cannot always connect our feelings to what is going on in the world. But there is no question that we know how we feel. The sun may be shining, the birds may be singing, and we may have just received wonderful news, but there is no telling how we really feel internally. The response to this may be one of flowing happiness, and then when we paint we are able to share this feeling with others through our brilliant colors, through our love of light, through the joy that comes into the painting. But, on the other hand, given the same set of circumstances on another day, we may paint what we intensely feel: a dark and brooding picture.

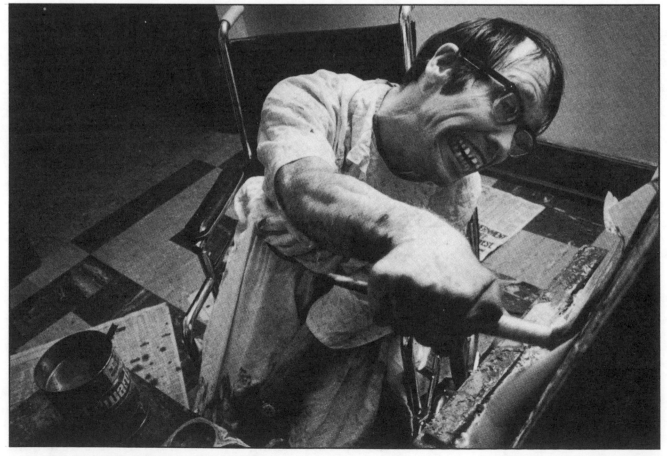

BILL ROAM - CREATIVE GROWTH

What would existence be like if suddenly the creative urge and its resultant expression were eliminated? How could there be progress and change without the creation of things new and different?

How dark and bleak the world would be if we all marched to the same tune, if we all had to fit a precise mold. It is only when the person is truly creative that he can fly and spin and sing and cry, "I am myself, I am unique, I am man."

Creativity of People with Disabilities

Given the premise that all people have the need and the right to develop their own creative expression, questions arise. Does a person who is disabled, who has been deprived, who has never had the opportunity to express himself still retain the essence of creativity? Does he still retain the joy of becoming a creative person? Does he still have the power to produce works of art that will be satisfying to himself and will have the power to move others?

Having been involved with creative Art Centers for people with disabilities for many years, we have no such questions. When the opportunity exists, we have seen the creative impulse burst forth like a surge of flood water when the dam has been removed. We have seen people cry when viewing their own work. We have seen the joy in their faces. We have seen the supreme effort made by their bodies to respond to their creative needs. We have seen "great" artists beg for paintings made by our students to hang in their own studios for inspiration. We have seen and we believe.

2 Creative Art, Art Therapy, Art in Recreation, Art Education

It is important to clarify the differences and similarities between creative art and art therapy, art in recreation and art education. One of the outstanding similarities is that all use art materials, art language, and personnel with art training. The striking differences are that each is distinct in its central ideas and its hoped for achievements.

Creative Art

Creative self-expression is the outward manifestation in an artistic form of what one feels internally. This expression may find its outlet in painting, sculpture, music, dance, poetry, or many other forms. It may be inspired by what one sees or experiences in the environment or a transformation of it; or it may be a reaction to inner moods, feelings, or sensations.

The essence of this definition is that creativity lies within the individual and is manifested in a distinctive type of aesthetic expression. Although there is a terrific drive for sharing, it is not necessarily a part of the creative act.

Art Therapy

The essence of art therapy is that it must partake of both parts of its name—it must involve art and therapy. The goal of the art activity, therefore, must be primarily therapeutic. This might, of course, include diagnosis as well as treatment; for in order to be an effective therapist, you must understand who and what you are treating. In order to be an effective *art* therapist, you must know a great deal about both components of this hybrid discipline. You must know *art*: the media and processes and their nature and potential. You must know the creative process, the language of art, and the nature of the symbol, form and content. You must also know *therapy*. You need to know about yourself and about others in terms of development, psychodynamics, and interpersonal relations. And you must know about the nature of the treatment relationship and the underlying mechanisms that help others to change.

— Judith A. Rubin (1982)

Art in Recreation

The primary motivation in a recreational art program is to stimulate people to use their leisure time in a profitable and enjoyable manner by participating in art activities. The person looks forward to the art experience as an after-school, after-work, or vacation activity. To many people, recreational art activities may be the most significant part of their lives.

Recreational art programs are most often available in summer camps, community centers, senior citizen centers, and city or county park and recreation facilities.

Art in Education

In education, art programs have different goals and methods. Three of the most important are described briefly below:

Art as a School Subject. Art is taught as a subject in the curriculum. As such, it is confined to a particular time of the day or week. The subject varies greatly—it may be art appreciation, art history, learning to draw, paint or sculpt, or learning any of the crafts. Some teachers use art lessons as a creative or enrichment experience.

The "Art-Infused" Curriculum. The art-infused curriculum has as its main goal the use of art activities for the improvement of general and specific learning and the enrichment of other subject matter being taught. For example, in the study of history, drawing a Roman feast may make the life of the Romans more understandable. In biology, drawing a flower may make it easier to understand the parts of a flower and their functioning. In arithmetic, the concept of "four" may be made easier when four apples are drawn. Art activities are carried on within the classroom and are usually integrated with academic subject matter. Much learning takes place when the child actively participates and becomes personally involved in art activities. In the art-infused curriculum, art is not necessarily taught as a creative experience.

Learning Through Art. According to Elliot Eisner (1985):

> . . . the arts are not only important because of what they represent, they are important because of the ways in which they engage and develop human intellectual ability. To learn to see and to make visual form is a complex and subtle task. The child needs to learn how to look, not simply assign a label to what is seen, but to experience the qualities to which he attends. Artistic tasks, unlike so much of what is now taught in schools, develop the ability to judge, to assess, to experience a range of meanings that exceed what we are able to say in words. The limits of language are not the limits of our consciousness. The arts, more than any other area of human endeavor, exploit this human capacity.

3 The Flourishing of Creativity

We have seen many people change and grow when they begin to create art, and continue to grow as they work. We would like to share some of our experiences.

George

George is a man in his sixties who spent most of his life in a state institution for the mentally retarded. He is blind in one eye, has a large tumor in his neck, shuffles when he walks, and seems completely disconnected from the world. He can say a few words but it is hard to know how much he comprehends since he mumbles when he talks and is difficult to understand.

George was sent to the Art Center because there was no other community program for him. When he was first placed at an art table, he put a few dabs of paint in one color on his paper and immediately returned to sitting on a couch on the side of the studio with his hands clasped on his head. He was placed back at the table. After a few weeks, to our surprise, his dots became lines and he retreated to the couch less frequently. After a few months the lines became areas and he began to use a number of colors. He learned to say our names and no longer retreated to the couch. His progress has continued. He developed his own style—paintings made of series of squares and rectangles using three or four colors. He delights in his work. As soon as he finishes his lunch he returns to the painting table and says he is going to work.

Recently George's work, when presented with a number of other students' work, was singled out by a gallery owner as being among the most promising. Of course George still exhibits many of the signs of his years in the institution, but his extreme interest in his work is apparent to all who visit the program.

Mary

Mary is a large buxom lady in her thirties. She lived with her mother, who took care of her every need. Her schooling was erratic. When her mother died, her social worker tried her in different programs, in each of which she failed. She made one last attempt, and brought her to the Art Center.

Mary delighted in making little pencil drawings of people. It seemed she had done these to while away the time at home. Then she added color to them. Gradually the drawings became paintings of people in many different aspects. Her brother is a bus driver and she drew his bus with all its passengers.

At present her work continues to become more colorful and more complex. She is not satisfied with working five days a week, six hours a day in the Center. She takes her work home to do art evenings and weekends.

She is extremely religious and her paintings very often show Mary, the Wise Men, Jesus, and stories from the Bible. Mary has discovered books and magazines such as the National Geographic. Suddenly Egyptian figures peopled her paintings together with palm trees and desert scenes.

Since she draws so much and is interested in detail, Mary was introduced to felt markers

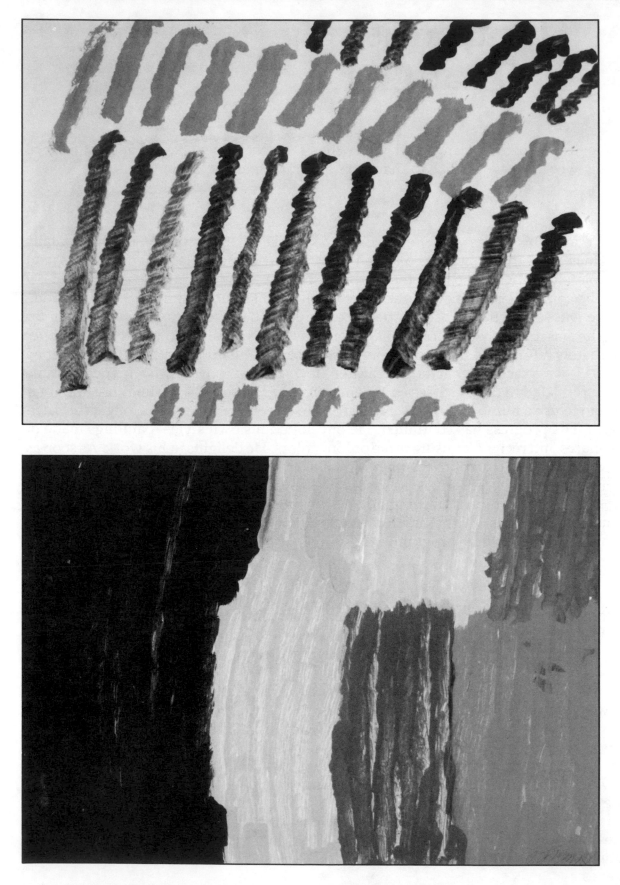

TWO STAGES IN THE DEVELOPMENT OF GEORGE SMITH

and craypas. She also enjoys drawing in black and white, even though her color is so rich and vibrant.

From the sale of her work, she has been able to purchase fine quality drawing materials.

James

James is a slender young man who has been discharged from every program he has attended. He is very retarded, but presents himself as one who understands everything. No matter what he is told, his answer is "I know." Because of this attitude, it is difficult to teach him.

He is a natural colorist with a completely individual style. His concepts are primitive, but he has the ability to place incongruous shapes and colors which somehow work together. Although little teaching can be done, encouragement and stimulation have led to brilliant paintings of the most fascinating quality. He is very difficult to get along with and presents behavior problems. However, he regularly attends the program, working continually and proudly. His work has been shown in many places and because of his originality, his work is the favorite of many artists and critics.

Sylvia

Sylvia is a young lady with Down Syndrome who was sent to the Art Center until a vacancy could be found in an adult social development program for severely limited persons. She took to painting, sculpture, and printmaking with incredible ability.

The joy she found in this form of expression is a delight to all who meet her. When a place opened for her in the social development center, her social worker wished to place her there but she and her mother refused to make the change. As her mother says, "Sylvia lives for her art and cannot wait until Monday rolls around so she can return to her art."

Her work is extremely complex and she works in different styles, all being consistent in the use of brilliant color with an intuitive sense of organized design. Her favorite methods of painting consist of mazes or grids of color, monoprints from free and splashy paintings, and heads that are part human and part spider and sun. Sylvia's work is very popular and people buy her work for the delightful freedom, color, and imagination.

We could go on and on, endlessly citing the joy and growth when disabled people are involved in the arts. We recognize the changes that take place not only in the person, but in family attitudes. Persons who were regarded as unproductive are now seen as productive citizens by their families and by the community. The self-image of these persons has changed from a dependent personality to feelings of positive self-esteem and worth.

Parents now introduce their adult children with such statements as "I would like you to meet my daughter, the artist!"

To come to the Art Center, to see the seriousness and intensity of the students as they are involved in creating art is a revelation to all who visit. But even more exciting is the prodigious amount of exceptionally fine art that is produced.

4 A Creative Visual Art Center for Disabled Adults

Even though a human being may be handicapped or disabled—mentally, physically or emotionally—this does not change his need to fulfill himself to the greatest of his capacity. On the contrary, this need is of even greater importance. The environments to which handicapped people are exposed—hospitals, sheltered workshops, family care homes, convalescent centers—often lack stimulation and provisions for growth and self-fulfillment. Disabled people need a place which enables them to fulfill and release their creative potential and to experience themselves as unique and worthwhile individuals.

The Art Center and Community Day Programs for Disabled Adults

Over the past forty years the number of day programs for disabled adults has greatly increased. There are many reasons for this. A major reason is the large-scale transfer of persons with mental, physical, and emotional problems from large, remote, often dismal state institutions to community residential facilities. Further, fewer people are being sent to state institutions. Most important has been the growing awareness by the general public that adults with disabilities can live more fruitful, independent and productive lives if they are provided with appropriate programs in the community.

Although these day programs vary greatly, they fall broadly into two categories. "Developmental" or "activity" programs are oriented toward recreation and socialization experiences appropriate for the severely disabled low functioning individual. "Sheltered workshops," "work activity centers," "rehabilitation centers," etc. are for higher functioning disabled adults who "work" on simple tasks under close supervision and earn hourly wages commensurate with their work productivity.

The Art Center for adults with disabilities is a new type of program designed primarily to meet the needs of disabled adults for creative self-expression in the arts. These Centers can also provide pre-vocational and vocational training in art and art-related fields. In this environment lower and higher functioning persons can work side by side, focusing on their creative work and intent on expressing themselves, regardless of the type or severity of the disability. The Art Center also offers opportunities to socialize during lunch, on breaks, or on trips and visits to art-related places.

Art Center students benefit tremendously from their experiences in the program, regardless of age or disability. Their feelings of self-worth improve and others begin to see them in a new light. In some instances they can earn money through the sale of their art work. The more able members can be trained to earn partial or total self-support through paid employment as Art Aides or assistants in art print shops.

Art Centers for persons with disabilities are an important innovative day program which should be a part of the array of services available to all adults with disabilities. Adults with disabilities who have not been able to function adequately in sheltered workshops or activity programs have found the Art Center a place where they feel fulfilled. We have worked with persons who have not attended other day programs and have profited greatly from the Art Center. We believe there are many persons with disabilities in every community who could profit from being in an Art Center, if such programs are made available.

The strengths of people with disabilities can be brought out only if there are opportunities. Art Centers help these persons fulfill themselves and become contributors to society. Especially in times like these when they are already denied so many opportunities, we must not do away with their rights to express themselves as human beings, nor can we compromise principles and ideals. There is no better time than the present to follow through on this philosophy.

Definition of a Creative Art Center for Adults with Disabilities

We define a visual Art Center for adults with disabilities as a full-time supportive and stimulating environment without pressure, threat, or competitiveness in which creative work in painting, sculpture, printmaking, creative crafts, etc. is carried on in a studio setting by people with mental, physical, or social disabilities. Both the creative process and the resultant art products are of great importance. In this setting great changes in personality, behavior and productivity often occur.

Such a Center may include other elements such as a gallery, a teaching program, outings, exhibitions, and any activity which will help achieve the goal of promoting the creativity of these persons.

Art Centers can take many forms. An Art Center can include all the expressive arts, such as music, dance, drama, visual arts, poetry, film, etc. An Art Center can take two or more of the arts and handle them as an integrated form, such as drama and costume design, or it may combine music and dance. An Art Center can also specialize in one of the arts.

We have chosen to write about visual Art Centers since this is our area of expertise and we have been working in this field for many years. There are many facets of specialization within the visual arts, such as painting, sculpture, printmaking, drawing, collage, assemblage, mosaics, murals, photography, weaving—enough to keep a person involved for a lifetime!

The Unique Contributions of a Creative Art Center

What does such a Center have to offer that makes it unique and important? The emphasis on creativity and self-expression in the visual arts promotes individual development and supports basic human aspirations for freedom and order. A nurturing and nondirective environment without emphasis on competition promotes growth and self-confidence. The act and results of creating serve as catalysts in mobilizing the different strengths in the person, and in welding these strengths together to form a total productive personality.

The Creative Art Center for people with disabilities is a new type of facility. Since it is still in its infancy there are many misconceptions and a lack of clarity about its distinctive qualities. The Creative Art Center sees each person, no matter how disabled mentally, physically, or emotionally, as a potential artist and seeks to develop the ability to create and to grow through rich and varying art experiences within a supportive environment. Disabilities are not viewed as illness (as in the "medical model") but as obstacles which can be overcome.

The Art Center is an open studio where people work at their own pace without pressure, with materials they choose and where teachers act as helpers or facilitators when needed. Growth in art and in the total person takes place through the student's own wish to fulfill his inner needs and to communicate with others through his art. There is no time-limited period of attendance since there is no end to creativity and to growth.

Attending the Art Center is very unlike attending an art class. The Art Center requires full commitment to its program. The expectations are of growth and development of the individual both in his art and as a person.

Participation in art classes is much less intensive. The primary function is either recreational or instructional. The classes are usually offered in schools, senior centers, community centers, park and recreation facilities, museums, etc. Classes are limited to one or two hours a week and students register for one or two classes. Many persons without disabilities as well as those with disabilities attend these classes for their personal enjoyment and education.

Goals of the Center

Each Center must formulate its goals as early as possible, in order to form a clear vision for future accomplishments. A statement of goals is essential as a guide for the Board of Directors, the Director, the staff, and for obtaining support in the community. It is necessary that the goals be clearly stated goals since evaluation of the Center is based on achievement of the goals. We propose the following goals as appropriate to a Creative Art Center:

Artistic development. Art Centers seek to provide an environment in which persons with disabilities can grow and can experience joy and fulfillment through creative self-expression. As the student works he changes and progresses. Each stage has its own characteristics and excitement. There is no limitation to what level of expressive accomplishment a person can achieve.

Creation of work of the highest artistic merit. Each person, no matter how limited intellectually, emotionally, or physically, is capable of artistic achievement at some level. The Center staff must always help these persons strive towards the highest quality the person can achieve. Remarkable and unforeseen results often happen. Work worthy of hanging in art galleries and museums is often produced.

Integration of the personality through creative experiences in the visual arts. All people can benefit from creative self-expression. The act of creating serves as a catalyst in mobilizing different strengths in the person to form a total productive personality.

Enhancement of self-image and self-esteem. Through their ability to express themselves people develop a positive self-image as worthwhile human beings. They take pride in their art and enjoy sharing their work with others. There is so little place in their lives where they can be proficient and feel successful. Failure, frustration and isolation are an everyday affair. Recognition bestowed by peers and the community adds to the joy and satisfaction of the artist and makes him feel a valued member of society.

Strengthening of ability to make decisions for oneself. Each person is encouraged to perform to the best of his capacity. The environment is noncompetitive and nonjudgmental. Making decisions is encouraged and respected. Each student must constantly make artistic choices as to subject matter, size, color arrangement, design, and techniques. An artist may complete work in 10 minutes or in three weeks. The work produced is his own. He has the right to fail and to try again. He may discard his work, leave it in the Center, or take it home. Other choices must also be made, e.g., how many days per week to come to the Center and what space to use while working.

Expression of inner feelings and moods. Being able to express internal conflicts, dreams and fantasies serves as a catharsis and helps to resolve feelings that otherwise would remain internalized with the potential of causing deviant behavior.

Improvement of communication skills. Each person is encouraged to express himself not only in his creative art work but in verbal communication. This leads to better interaction with those around him, his peers, the staff and the volunteers.

Improvement of coordination and use of equipment and tools. All the visual arts require that the image be implemented through eye and hand coordination in the use of tools such as pencils, pens, chisels, brushes, etc. If it is impossible to use the hands, other parts of the body such as the mouth or toes must be called upon to act as substitutes.

Development of potentials for independent living. There is room for growth in self-sufficiency in all people. Increasing independence at any level has far-reaching effects on the total personality and behavior.

Prevocational training and experiences. Certain basic competencies essential for all persons are particularly stressed, such as concentration on task, understanding of limits, self-motivation, self-discipline, and cooperation with others. In addition, habits such as personal cleanliness, cleaning up after work, punctuality, regular attendance and appropriateness of dress are also essential for future employment.

Vocational training and experiences. In some instances students may be capable of being trained in art skills that will lead to part-time or full-time jobs. Students have been trained and placed in paid employment as art aides in convalescent hospitals and in art classes for handicapped children and adults. Capable students can also be trained as helpers in art print shops and in other art-related fields. The training must be thorough and individualized to suit each student's capabilities. There must be follow-up and support to help the disabled person maintain these jobs.

Marketing of art. It is extremely appropriate for the Art Center to sell the art work of the students. The students gain by feeling their art is worthy of being bought and perhaps reproduced. The money is a welcome addition to the praise of a job well done. The Art Center takes pride in the recognition that the art of persons with disabilities is much sought after and has value to society. The marketing of art should be done in a professional and dignified way, using persons with experience in this field who are sensitive to the creativity of the work.

Prevention of inappropriate institutionalization. Capability for remaining in the community depends on being able to adapt to the environment. Providing them with a program of personal development, artistic growth and satisfaction gives the community a chance to see them as worthwhile people deserving community acceptance.

Involvement of families, caretakers, social agencies. Students live in homes, are involved with their families or with caretakers, and are supervised by and known to many social agencies. In order to be of greatest benefit to the student and to others who serve him, constant communication with all his significant contacts must be maintained. In this way it is possible to plan for the whole person.

Active participation of the community, volunteers, interns, and students. Volunteers, including students and interns doing field work in social work, special education, psychology, recreation and art are actively solicited. Their participation is important as a normalizing model. They, in turn, gain much from this experience. Students in training represent a pool of potential professional workers in this field.

Involvement of children and youth with disabilities. Although children and teenagers cannot attend an Art Center full time since they are going to school, they can attend part time or Saturdays. It is important for children to become involved in the arts at an early age since this will often lead to a continuing interest throughout their lives. It is especially important for children with disabilities since many of their options are limited by physical and mental problems. In art, these limitations can vanish and they are equal with all other children.

Education of the general public through exhibits, publications, seminars, workshops. The Center has a public education function, not only for the general public but for legislators, educators, artists, and other professionals. It is an advocate for a cause—the creativity of people with disabilities. The Center constantly exhibits the creative art work of the students. It conducts workshops and conferences, prepares and circulates posters and publications, and communicates with the public through newspapers, magazines, radio and TV. An art gallery showing the students' work under professional standards, integrated with the art work of practicing artists, adds much to public appreciation and understanding.

Rationale for a Separate Art Center for People with Disabilities

Under ideal conditions it would not be necessary to establish a separate Art Center for persons with disabilities. They should be integrated into existing art programs, art schools and art experiences and not be separated from others because of their disabling conditions. Their special needs should be provided for in integrated settings. Since the great majority of these persons are still not admitted to existing facilities, because of the many negative attitudes towards them and the cost of modifications necessary to accommodate them, it becomes imperative to establish a separate Art Center.

It is our dream that ultimately such special facilities will not be needed and all people will be able to work together toward the highest fulfillment of each individual and of society as a whole. At present the Art Center attempts to integrate as much as possible by having nondisabled volunteers working side by side with the artist-students with disabilities, by showing their work alongside nondisabled artists, by entering juried shows, by having special events with all people invited, by welcoming visiting artists, and by making trips to art exhibits, art events, and artist's studios.

Rationale for an Independent Art Center for People with Disabilities

An Art Center for people with disabilities can be established as an independent organization or as part of a larger organization. After working in many different settings, we have come to the conclusion that an *independent* Art Center is the most effective format. An independent Center with its own Board of Directors is able to clearly define what it proposes to do and can seek the funds and personnel to achieve its goals. It is not subject to rules and demands which can arbitrarily be imposed by a parent organization. It can demonstrate visibly to donors and prospective contributors exactly what benefits are being provided to art students in the program, and it can demonstrate the accomplishments of the students when exposed to such a setting.

It provides a creative art environment not subject to or diluted by other demands. Students know what the program is and what is expected of them and respond with joy and courage. Highly qualified professional artist-teachers, volunteers, and interns are attracted by this philosophy.

Description of an Independent Art Center for People with Disabilities

Art is best produced in an environment which stimulates the imagination. There should be a studio atmosphere of freedom to create which is nonjudgmental and noncompetitive. The space should be large, light, uncrowded and flexible, with no constraints of preconceived neatness and conformity. Floors should be concrete or linoleum, which are easy to maintain and pose no cleaning problems. Every section should be easily accessible to all persons, no matter how severely handicapped.

Experimentation with many tools, materials and ideas should be encouraged. An abundance of inexpensive supplies should be available: paper in a variety of sizes and colors, cardboard, wood scraps, wool, clay, different types of chalks, crayons, paints, etc. There should be no limitation on the use of color, materials, style or size of work. A kiln and art press should be provided.

Students should be able to make the choice of working on tables, on the floor, or on easels. Only the artist knows what is comfortable for him.

Learning through experience, especially in the arts, is essential for each person to explore and develop his own individuality, ideas, and unique approaches and methods.

It is essential to have trained art teachers, since in every art student's growth there is a time when he feels the need for instruction in techniques which only a well-trained art instructor can provide. The staff is there to help students develop according to their own needs and inclinations. The teacher's job is one of stimulation and encouragement and to be available when needed for teaching special skills.

Never should the teacher become the dominant force. The learning of specific techniques should be considered secondary to the joy and desire of creating and to the excitement of discovery and fulfillment of the creative act.

In this type of environment, where limitations are minimal, it may at first seem that students will abuse their privileges. For those of us who have worked with students using this philosophy we have found the exact opposite. They enjoy what they are doing. They stay with their work and are motivated to investigate. They progress at their own rate. They learn to respect their work and the work of others. They learn the possibilities and limitations of the materials. With involvement in work and a growing sense of accomplishment, with the interest of the staff and the community, students develop and change. Why it happens we do not know, but it happens. Students begin to take control of themselves. There is a difference when discipline is imposed by external forces such as the staff and when discipline evolves from the person's need for order and organization in dealing with a free environment. Self-image and self-esteem as well as the ability to deal with their own problems grow and they feel themselves persons of worth. This feeling transmits itself to their total personality and to their total functioning as human beings and as creative artists.

There is no one way of developing and structuring an Art Center. Each will be individual, according to local needs, available funding, disabling conditions, ethnic make-up, the expertise, experience and philosophy of the Board of Directors, the Director, and the staff. Some

Centers concentrate on one of the arts, such as painting, while others include several arts. *The basic commonality is the focus on creativity, the belief that all persons can grow in many dimensions, can enjoy themselves, and can produce work of high artistic quality*

II.
The Living Arts Center

Chapters 5-11

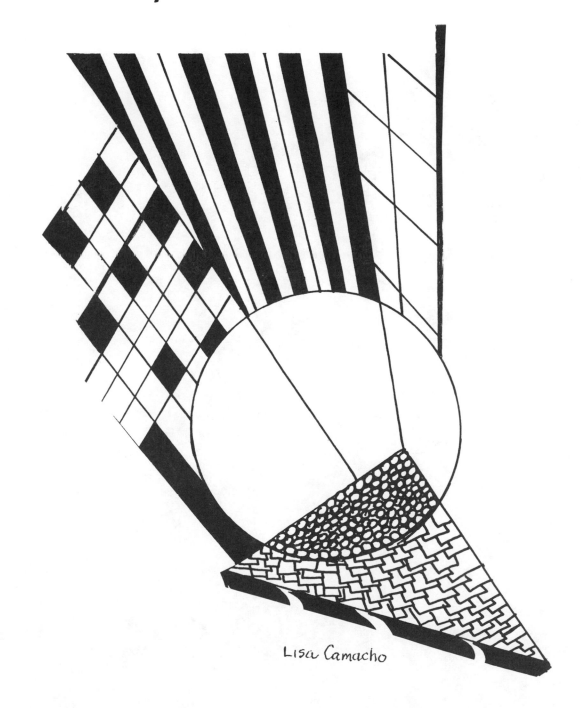

Lisa Camacho

5 Philosophy of Teaching Art

The primary goal of the art teacher is to help develop creative persons who experiment with many images, ideas, materials, and techniques. Art for the student should be an enjoyable, releasing, and challenging experience. Technical proficiency should be secondary to expressive power. The student should feel a sense of accomplishment. His work should be important to himself and he should feel that it is important to others.

The art will vary according to the needs of the students, their background and experiences, their physical and ethnic characteristics, local cultural interests, available funds, and the expertise of the teaching staff.

Although the Art Center is very flexible in its teaching, certain principles cannot be compromised.

Credo for Art Teachers

An art teacher's primary function is to stimulate the students, to implant in them a desire, an urge to create. It is for the teacher to help release the excitement that exists in all of us when we are able to express our feelings, our thoughts, our images. The success of the teacher is measured by the students' absorption in their work and by their desire to continue. In this way true growth takes place. Often does a student's work through its integrity, through its power, through its rightness exceed the technically perfect work of the teacher.

No matter how immaturely the student works, even if it is merely scribbling, he should be allowed to work at his own speed. Many students have never had the experience of going past the scribble stage and must be given the opportunity to work through it and develop further. Even if a student never gets beyond the scribble stage but continues to be absorbed by what he is doing, the teacher should be willing to accept this mode of expression. This does not mean that the teacher cannot make suggestions, but the teacher should not force the student to follow them nor should he deprecate the student's artistic attempts.

Each student's work must be genuinely the work of the student. A teacher should never work on a student's piece unless it is understood to be a joint work and is labeled as such.

Students should be allowed to select the media and subject matter. Teachers may suggest a variety or change in subject and media to expand the horizons of the student but never demand that the student conform. Art work should be original works created by the student. A teacher should never give a student a picture to replicate by copying, tracing or filling in, or a mold from which to make a cast. This is an easy way to get results but it does not answer the creative needs of the student nor does it add to his artistic development.

Each student should learn to work to the best of his or her abilities. Art is not a competitive activity. A teacher should not hold up another student's work as a model towards which a student should strive. A teacher should never tell a student that his work is better or worse than the work of another student. Comparisons are odious.

Teachers should use a positive approach to a student's work. Criticism should be constructive. Any negative remarks should always be accompanied by suggestions of how to improve the work and by pointing out the parts of the work which are well done.

The student should learn to make independent judgments in art. At all times the teacher should seek to preserve and enlarge the creativity of the student. Never should he allow his own creative urges to dominate or supersede the creativity of the student. The teacher should never make a student dependent on the teacher, on another student, or on copying.

The teacher should encourage a student to take new steps and should help with technical problems. However, if the project becomes too difficult, it should be eliminated before frustration takes over. The prime goal is not to produce highly technically skilled artisans but creative people.

There are many ways to create a work of art or to solve aesthetic problems. The teacher should never assume that there is "only one right way"—the teacher's way.

A student has the right to fail and try again.

Artist-Teachers Speak

After having taught for half a century, I believe that art as such cannot be taught, but a lot can be done to open eyes and mind to meaningful form. Teaching can prepare a readiness to reveal and evoke insight.

Josef Albers*

You can teach art but you can't make an artist. People talk about academic training. I can only say that the word "academic" has had very little meaning in my artistic life.

Hans Hoffman*

I had an academic background—studied and drew from the model. I don't really know whether this is important or not. There's a lot of stuff you've learned that you've got to eliminate as you go along. I happen to like drawing. I can't very well estimate how much my training helped me. I suppose what you've really got to do is learn pretty much everything yourself. After all, what you finally do is a decision only you can make. If anyone would have told me that at forty I would be painting only in black and white, I wouldn't have believed it. These things happen slowly.

Franz Kline*

Rarely can there be found a scribbling or babbling that is not a direct expression of a mental and emotional state. However, more complete forms of art expression can be easily influenced by stronger personalities. This influence often grows to such an extent that complex forms of art, even in spite of technical perfection, may lack completely the inner spirit or the mental and emotional state of the creator.

Viktor Lowenfeld**

* Josef Albers, Hans Hofmann, and Franz Kline are quoted from Katherine Kuh, *The Artist's Voice*, New York: Harper and Row, 1961.

**Viktor Lowenfeld is quoted from Viktor Lowenfeld and W. Lambert Brittain, *Creative and Mental Growth*, New York: Macmillan Co., 1964 (4th Edition).

6 The Art Studio of a Creative Art Center

To illustrate how a Creative Arts Center works, we describe the Creative Art Studio of a functioning Art Center. It is housed in a residential neighborhood of middle and low income homes. The Studio occupies 4,000 square feet of the Art Center's 8,700 square feet. It is located adjacent to a park and is light, airy, and comfortable, though somewhat crowded. The building is ramped and there are no physical or architectural barriers to the movement of persons with disabilities. It is accessible by public transportation.

Most students come daily for six-hour sessions. Some attend other programs two or three days a week. Programming is individual and flexible according to the desire and needs of each individual. The Studio is run as an open studio with each artist-student working at his own pace on work of his own choosing. There are many experiences to choose—painting, drawing, collage, sculpture, clay modeling, printmaking, and weaving. On certain days some of the students, accompanied by a teacher, go on field trips to museums, galleries, artists' studios, or on sketching trips.

Visitors, volunteers, interns, and college students are welcome to observe and participate in the program.

A Typical Day of a Student in the Creative Art Studio

David uses public transportation and has learned to make two changes from his home to the Studio. He arrives at 9:30 a.m. and signs in. He writes unintelligibly, but the staff has learned to recognize his signature. He hangs up his coat, puts his lunch box away, and puts on his smock.

The art teachers have been there for an hour and have prepared art supplies, consisting of tempera paints, water colors, colored pens, sculpture, and printing materials. These are placed on different tables around the room. Papers of all sizes and colors are stored in easily accessible open cabinets.

The work David does is determined by his own desire. He may be stimulated by the materials he sees in front of him or by images he saw on the way to the studio or by a dream or a vision. He may have an idea for a new work or he may be continuing an unfinished one. He makes his own decision as to where he wishes to work. There is no seat assigned to him. This morning he chooses to work on an unfinished painting.

He cannot immediately find his picture. An art teacher helps him go through a small stack of unfinished work. He picks out his painting, looks around the room and sees a friend he would like to work next to. He goes to the table and places his paper on it. He walks around the room, finds the colors and brushes he needs, and places them on the table in front of him. He is now ready for work.

David works intently, stopping in mid-morning for a juice break. The teachers occasionally stop to talk with him. They offer suggestions but *do not demand that he comply with them.* David will make his own decision as to whether he wishes to carry out their suggestions or if he wishes to proceed in his own way. A little before lunch, he is finished with his painting. He asks a teacher to look at it and discuss it with him. The teacher makes suggestions and David decides to make some minor changes. When he is finished to his own satisfaction, he places the painting on the drying rack. Since he cannot write, the teacher helps him sign his name and the date.

He decides to go to the clay table. He places clay on a bat and now it is the beginning of the lunch hour. He takes his lunch box and goes to the area where the other students are gathering for lunch. Coffee and juice are available. He brings only a skimpy sandwich. A staff member makes a mental note of this lunch and will bring it up later during a staff case discussion of David and his work.

David finishes his lunch in 15 minutes and decides to look at art books and art magazines. Since he does not have a clean-up assignment on this day, when the other students are finished with lunch he goes to the park and plays kick ball with them until the end of lunch hour.

After lunch hour, he returns to the clay table and starts modeling a head. He has trouble adhering the nose to the form he has built. He approaches a teacher and points out his problem. The teacher gets clay of his own and shows him how to score and use slip to make connections. David practices this and when he has mastered the technique under the teacher's guidance, he returns to his sculpture and applies the knowledge he has gained. He is dissatisfied with the first results and starts again. The teacher comes by a little later to see how he is doing and shows him how to improve his technique.

A volunteer becomes interested in what David is doing. She gets her own clay and sits next to him. They share their discoveries.

A teacher walks by, stops to speak to David, who proudly displays what he has learned. He continues working on the head.

A few minutes before 3:30 p.m. it is clean-up time. David puts wet cloths on the head and places it where the unfinished clay work is kept. Tomorrow he will be able to continue. He cleans the table where he has worked and puts away his tools. He hangs up his smock, says goodbye, and leaves for the day.

This picture of David shows a self-sufficient, interested person able to care for himself, to make decisions, to travel independently. He is able to ask for and take assistance and criticism in an appropriate manner and is completely involved in his work. He is able to work independently as an artist.

This was not always the case. When David first came to the Center after many years of institutionalization he could not travel independently. He could not pronounce his name distinctly. Unless he was explicitly told where to go and what to do, he stood in a corner and rocked. Although he still has many areas of difficulty, he is now a happy, dependable man and a promising artist. What caused this great change?

Although he is a man with great talents in many different fields of the visual arts, his talent did not show immediately. His first paintings were childish and without imagination, very like the drawings in a coloring book. Very likely he had spent many hours coloring pictures while in the institution. His subject matter was pumpkins, four-leaf clovers, Mickey Mouse and Bugs Bunny drawings. Gradually the work changed. Hills, mountains and buildings seen en route to the Center and people he knew began to appear in his pictures. Less time was spent rocking in the corners and more time absorbed in his work. He no longer had to be told where to go and what to do.

In his work, new developments started. He began to model with clay—at the beginning a primitive head, followed by astounding portraits of people in the Center. He discovered black and white drawing and spent much time designing pages for calendars and publications. An artist came to demonstrate weaving. David took to this immediately. He designed a hanging rug and was able to complete it with meticulous craftsmanship and sell it.

During this period of development he began to talk, very hesitantly and slowly, not always correctly, but he was able to make himself understood. Rocking almost totally disappeared since there was no longer any time or need for it.

The staff, after much discussion and concern, decided he could travel to the Studio by himself. He was encouraged to paint pictures of the restaurant where he would have to get off the bus, to draw the bus with its correct number, to draw the time on the clock when he had to leave home in the morning. Despite misgivings and mistakes, he finally learned. Now he travels by public transportation not only to the Studio, but to many other places.

What has happened to David is not unique. Many students go through a similar growth process and become capable artists and are recognized as such. Through creative experiences in art they learn to care for themselves, to travel, to speak more fluently, to become proud of their accomplishments. Their behavior reflects these changes. They earn money from the sale of their art work. They are contributing members of society and society is enriched by their efforts.

7 Art Media

In setting up the art studio, the Director should work closely with the art teachers, with specialists in art and disabilities, and with artists. Each Center develops its own methods of preparing the studio for use. Following is the method we have found most effective after years of experimentation.

When the Studio first opens and the students have had little or no experience, it would be wise to limit the art media to only two: tempera for painting and clay for sculpture. These are most universal in appeal, are easy to use, and offer immediate success. When the students have more experience, other media should be introduced slowly.

A student should take his time and get as much as he can from each experience. It can be disastrous if a student is pushed by the teacher to try new experiments before he is ready to give up accustomed ways. The student alone will know when he is ready and willing to take on new and challenging experiences.

Organizing and Adapting the Art Media

Following are a number of art experiences using different art media and suggestions of how to organize them effectively. This is by no means a comprehensive list, but serves as a guide in planning a program. Much experimentation will have to be done by the students and the teachers. New ways of using materials will be discovered. The organization and setup will be modified by each group.

After the Studio has been running smoothly, different tables are set up for various art work: tempera painting, watercolors, acrylics, collage, assemblage, clay work, drawing, printmaking, weaving, etc. The space for each art experience can be adjusted as needed.

PAINTING

Painting is one of the most important activities in the Art Studio. Painting takes many forms, but all types of painting are essentially the application of color to flat or three-dimensional surfaces. Paintings may be abstract, realistic or decorative, but all have in common the stimulation of the imagination and visual imagery through the use of color, texture, and design.

Tempera Painting

Tempera (poster color) is one of the simplest forms of paint to use. Liquid tempera comes already mixed in a great variety of colors. These colors can easily be combined to form an even greater number of colors. In our many years of experience, we have found few students who are unable to use a brush and tempera paint. When people have brilliant appealing colors and blank paper placed in front of them, we do not hear "What shall I do?". A brush is dipped into color and away the artist goes.

For tempera painting, two lunchroom tables (about 6 feet long and 30" wide) are placed

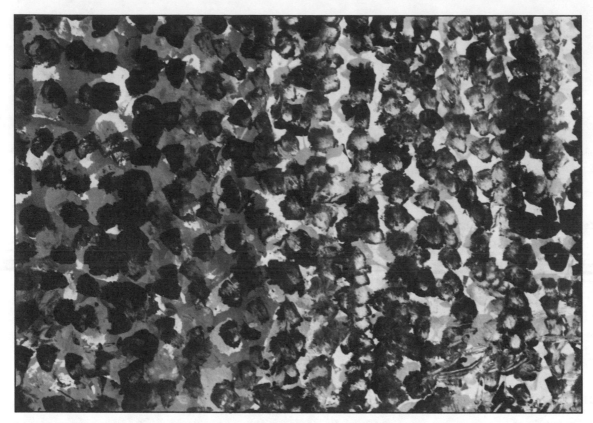

YELLOW & BLUE ABSTRACT — TEMPERA — SAMUEL GANT

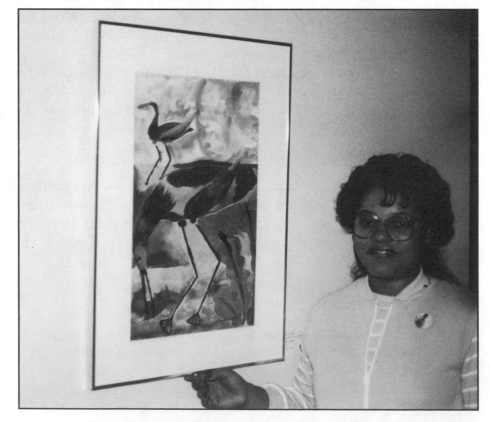

ANGELA CAMPBELL SHOWING HER WATER COLOR
AT THE RICHMOND ART CENTER JURIED EXHIBITION

together. In this way, students always face each other. Paints in baby food jars are placed in the center, with the paper along both sides. Students on either side of the table can use the paints without dropping them on the floor. There is ample room for each student to have his paper in front of him. Usually it is preferable to paint flat on the table so the paint does not drip. However, there are some students who prefer working on easels. Easels should be readily available.

It is a good idea for the art teacher to mix many different colors, values and intensities, and place them in jars on the tables beforehand so that the student on entering the studio will be stimulated by the colors. When colors are laid out in this way, students have a strong desire to use them. It is unbelievable what this set-up can do to stimulate even those who have had no previous desire to paint. We can liken it to a table that is heaped with tantalizing food—delightful in color and stimulating to the appetite.

Baby food jars are used for tempera or poster colors for many reasons. On the table the color glows through the glass, making a most inviting display. If the colors are sensitively mixed, it is hard to resist painting with them. The covers fit tightly on the jars so they can be stored at night and the glass is heavy enough and well-balanced so the jars do not tip over. They can be moved around the table and can be filled or cleaned individually. And best of all, they are free.

A brush should be placed in each jar so that the brush need not be washed when the student wishes to change to another color. He merely changes jars with the brush in it. This simplifies the procedure and also helps prevent colors from becoming muddy. Long brushes should have the handles cut so as not to turn the jars over.

If the student wishes to use a color which is not on the table, he either mixes it himself using a clean jar or he asks for help from the teacher.

When a student has finished a painting, he signs and dates it or asks the teacher's assistance. He then places his work on the floor or on a special rack for drying.

This method works exceedingly well for almost all people. However, there are some who, due to physical disabilities, may need special adaptations. Suggestions to enable them to work will be found in Appendix A. Suggestions for painting in tempera for the blind may also be found in Appendix A.

Tempera or poster color need not be expensive but should be brilliant, without much filler, which dulls the color. The consistency should be like that of sour cream—heavy enough not to run and thin enough to be easily spread.

There are four types of tempera or poster color—powder, liquid, cake, and tube. Powder paint is often used because of its apparent lower cost. However, when you consider the amount of filler in most powder paint, which results in poor color, and the valuable time and energy used by teachers in mixing the powder with water, it is not really a bargain. Tubes are difficult to handle and very often students need a teacher's assistance. Cakes can be used, but do not provide the freedom and flow of liquid tempera. We have found liquid tempera purchased in gallons most satisfactory and economical.

Brushes should be of different widths—1/4", 1/2", 3/4", and 1". Some very fine brushes should also be provided, as well as some 2" and 3" brushes. It is not necessary to have high quality brushes. However, they must be able to hold the paint without becoming limp or losing their hairs. Good utility or lacquer brushes can be found which serve adequately. Soft oil-painting brushes can also be used. If money is no object, water color brushes are excellent. Some brushes have long handles which have a tendency to unbalance the baby food jars, making them easy to knock over. These should be cut down to about eight inches. For special adaptations for people who have difficulty holding brushes, see Appendix A.

There are other tools besides brushes used in tempera painting. Paints can be spread over certain surfaces of the paper with cardboard or plastic pieces and then overlaid with other colors. Pointed sticks can be used to scratch and remove portions of paint. Printing with found objects such as spools, washers, textured papers, etc. can be done on the painted background. Students develop great skill in obtaining desired effects through these methods.

Paper for tempera painting should be in many sizes, the usual size being about 22" x 28". Some students prefer to paint on sheets about 10" x 14" while others prefer sheets as large as 40" x 60". Students should be encouraged to experiment with different sizes, textures, and shapes of paper.

The paper need not be expensive, but should be heavy enough not to disintegrate from the paint. For this reason newsprint is not a good choice for tempera. The paper should not be so slick that paint will not adhere. For sources of paper see Appendix B.

Although most people prefer to paint flat on the tables, some will prefer to work on easels. It is important that these should be provided for them. For some severely handicapped people, having tabletop or floor-standing easels in front of their wheelchairs may be the only way for them to paint. For very large paintings paper can be tacked to the walls, tacked to very large easels similar to the individual table easels, or can be spread on the floor. For adaptations for physically handicapped people, see Appendix A.

Water Color Painting

The setup for water color is not as exacting as for tempera painting. Since water color paints come in tubes or in small pans in a box, much of the visual excitement of seeing a glorious array of color is absent. It is important to keep water color boxes clean so that students will get stimulation from seeing the variety of colors.

In essence, the setup of tables with students on each side of the tables remains the same. It is essential that each student face another student so that communication may be established.

Each student has a box or tubes of water color, brushes, a jar of water (either glass or a coffee tin), some sort of small mixing tray or palette near the box so that the student can mix colors, a sponge to lift excess water or color, and a sheet of paper.

Although tube water color is usually preferred by artists, many students do not have the ability to unscrew the cap, press out the color, and screw the cap back on. For these students cake water color is the most practical way to go. Cake water color can be purchased in large cubes or in the classroom paint box. It is important to experiment to find out which type of water color is best suited for each student. Cheap children's sets with anemic color should never be used. This is not a saving, just a frustration.

Water color is much more difficult to use than tempera (poster, show card), since it requires more control. The technique of stroking and grading colors and adding the right amount of water is much more exacting than brushing on tempera paints directly from the jar. However, there are students who prefer using water colors and can handle them beautifully and sensitively. All students should have the experience at some time.

Different types and sizes of brushes, such as Japanese, soft-haired, stiff-haired, long-haired, and short-haired should be tried. A really good water color brush is an expensive tool and should be reserved for those who show real interest in working in this medium. Cheaper camel-hair brushes will serve adequately for most students. Brushes that have loose ferrules, that go limp in water, or lose their hairs, and round brushes that do not come to a point when used should never be purchased, no matter how inexpensive. Working with this type of inadequate tool is frustrating and leads to poor results. Before purchasing, always test water color brushes by dipping them into water. See if they come to a point and try how they react when stroking them on paper.

Brushes for water color should be kept separately from other brushes and should be used only for this medium.

Students should experiment with all kinds of papers, including oriental and domestic papers, since water colors on different papers produce entirely different effects. They should also have the experience of working on wet paper and on dry paper. Students are capable of making their own aesthetic judgments as to what pleases them after they have experimented sufficiently.

When a student reaches a proficient level of water color painting, he should have the experience of working on special paper made for water colors. Although this is expensive, best results are usually obtained by using water color paper, professional brushes, and good quality water color paint.

Finger Painting

Finger painting is certainly a legitimate method of painting. However, since we are dealing with adults who generally have low self-esteem and who have great difficulty in establishing themselves as mature capable people in the community, it is not particularly advisable to emphasize painting which for so long has been associated with children's painting. We seek at all times to maintain an adult image for our students, as capable of working in the same manner as any adult artist.

It is best to reserve finger painting for those who show special interest and desire. Certainly if a student wishes to get his fingers into the paint and move the paints around, he should not be prohibited or discouraged. Some students may show special interest in a combination of brush painting and then working with flat pieces of plastic, thin sticks, or with their fingers. Any method the student finds stimulating and comfortable and with which he can obtain results should not be discouraged.

Acrylic Painting

The setup for acrylics is much the same as for water colors. The colors are rich and vibrant. When painted on masonite or canvas, they give very much the same effect as oils. Many students feel they are producing "professional" works of art when they paint in acrylics.

Acrylics usually come in tubes or jars. If the Studio uses a great deal of acrylics, paint should be purchased in large jars. Acrylics are a much more expensive medium than tempera or water colors. There is a lot of spoilage because of quick drying. Many handicapped people find them difficult to handle. We have found it best to restrict their daily use to students who are interested in textural effects that cannot be obtained with other water-based paints.

All students who are capable of handling acrylics should have exposure and opportunity to experiment with them. Acrylics can be thinned with water and used on paper or can be used directly from the tube or jar as an impasto on cardboard, canvas, or masonite. A textural agent can be added to give the acrylics more body and texture. Acrylics can be easily mixed together to form a wide range of colors.

Brushes must be washed immediately and carefully, and not allowed to harden. Brushes of synthetic hair do not spoil as easily and are a good investment.

Oil Painting

Oil paints are expensive, difficult to clean, must be mixed with flammable solvents, and present health and fire hazards. Much the same effect can be obtained with acrylics. For the above reasons, unless a student ardently wishes to use oils, it is not a particularly good idea to use or store oil paints and solvents such as turpentine in the Studio.

Painting with Other Media

There are many materials, usually thought of as drawing materials, which can be used for painting. Among these are craypas, pastels, felt pens, color brush pens, crayons, etc. When these materials are used in a painterly fashion rather than for drawing and their main purpose is to color large areas, they can be considered as painting media.

DRAWING

Drawing is using a pencil, pen, crayon, felt tip marker, or chalk to make an abstract, decorative, or realistic image. A drawing may be made either in one color or in many colors.

Drawing and painting are not the same. Different interests and skills are involved. There are painters who are not particularly interested in drawing and artists who draw but who do not care to paint. Pencils are inexpensive, make no dirt, and are easy to handle. Pencils traditionally are used for drawing. For these reasons many disabled persons have never done any art form except drawing. We therefore find it better to start the student with a different medium so that old habits will not be reinforced. We feel that drawing with pencil may be better saved for a later experience, after other drawing materials have been tried. This does not mean that drawing with pencil is not a legitimate art experience and for some the most appropriate and exciting.

Drawing should be encouraged using such old standbys as pencils, pens, crayons, pastels, colored pencils, lithographic crayons, graphite, as well as the newer materials which include all sorts of felt and nylon tipped pens, brush pens, and craypas.

Drawings in black on white paper are the easiest form of art to reproduce. These drawings can be made with a variety of pens and india ink. For many disabled persons who are unable to control the ink, felt pens of all sizes can be used with excellent results. Drawings for reproduction may include specific subject matter for illustrating newsletters, articles for magazines, and newspapers or they may be abstract and decorative.

Drawings are very often made for tee shirts, brochures, announcements, posters, etc.

SCULPTURE

Sculpture is the act of creating three-dimensional forms from clay, wood, marble, metal, plastic, fiber or any other material or combination of materials. Sculpture may be abstract, decorative, or realistic. Sculpture may exist in three dimensions (sculpture in the round). It may project from a background (low or high relief) or it may be sunk into the background (intaglio). Sculpture may be conceived by cutting away from the background or it may be a combination of masses already in existence, such as found objects. Sculpture may be left in its natural state or it may be fired or painted.

Clay Sculpture

Clay is one of the most important materials for students to become familiar with. It is the most easily used and most responsive three-dimensional material. It allows students to create a finished object from raw material. It literally grows and takes shape before one's eyes. Almost all students have the ability to manipulate clay.

Clay can be rolled, flattened, squeezed, pinched, built up into forms, added to, subtracted from. Clay can be put together, cut apart, incised, decorated, textured. It can be made silky smooth or woolly rough.

It is very inviting if the student sees clay on the table when he enters the studio. The clay should be of a good consistency, responsive and pleasant to the touch. Clay can be placed in the center of the table, shaped in balls or cubes, or a large lump of clay can be placed near each student. Those who wish more clay should have access to a pail filled with clay.

Bats of plaster on which to work the clay can be easily made for each student. Pieces of plywood about 12" square are also excellent to work on. These bases enable the student to easily turn his sculpture while working. The work can be seen from all sides and can be lifted from the table when finished. "Lazy susans" which can often be purchased cheaply in salvage shops make it possible for students to turn their work even more easily.

The most direct method of working with clay is digging in with your hands and fingers the way children delight in playing with mud or wet sand. A ball of clay can be pinched, squeezed, and pressed into shapes. A student can form human and animal figures, abstract designs, bowls and pots using this method.

Another method is coiling clay. Pieces of clay can be rolled out with the palm of the hand and the fingers into fat and thin coils. Again, figures, animals, abstract forms and pottery shapes can be built from the coils.

Many students enjoy working clay by flattening out the clay into slabs. This is especially true of those who have been taught to be clean and "never make a mess." The easiest way to make slabs is by flattening clay with a rolling pin. The flattened clay can be cut into shapes or rolled into cylinders. Flat shapes can be used as tiles or plaques, or can be built into boxes, houses, etc. Cylinders can be used as vases, cups, and parts of a building. Combined shapes can be assembled into houses, flowers, boxes, and abstract forms.

It is important to teach the student how to adhere pieces of clay firmly. All individual pieces of a clay project must be scored and moistened before pressing them together, to make a permanent joining. Caution must be taken not to make the pieces so wet that they lose form. In our experience it has been helpful to place near each student a lid with water (this prevents overwetting) and a tool for scoring the clay.

With a severely handicapped group, it is best not to use a potter's wheel since the skill necessary often leads to frustration. However, if one is available it should be experimented with. There are students who do excellent work on the wheel. The abilities of people with disabilities are so diverse and so unpredictable that nothing can be taken for granted.

Clay can be decorated by pressing with tools and fingers. It can be incised with sharp points. Decorations can be built up by adding more clay or by carving into the clay. All the above methods can be combined and used in one clay piece.

Most art stores carry specialized tools for clay. However, many tools can be made at the Studio. Tongue depressors, popsicle sticks and dowels can be shaped into modeling tools. Heavy wire or hairpins attached to dowels by wire or strapping tape can be used for cutting the clay. Discarded dentists' tools are excellent. All sorts of gadgets can provide interesting textures.

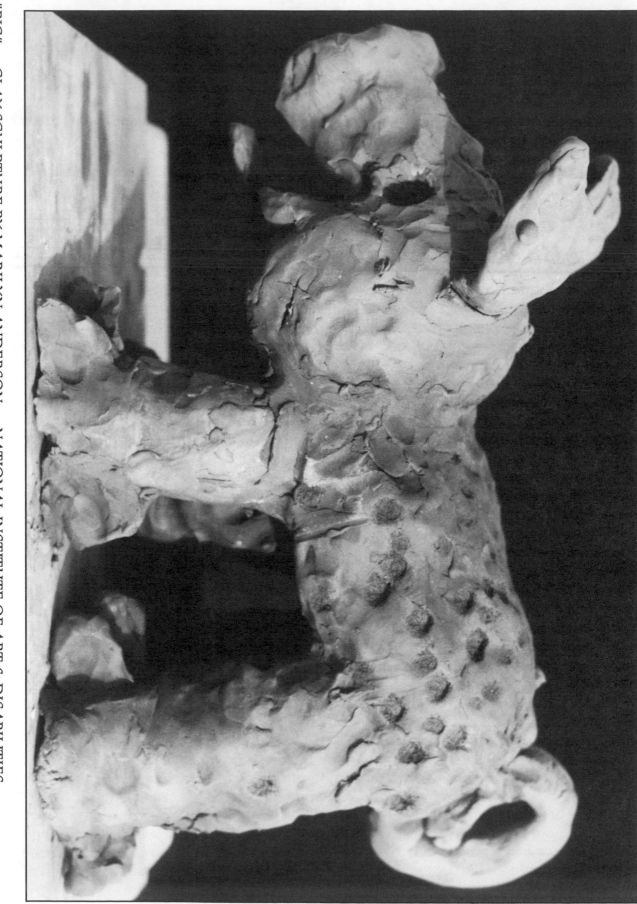

"PIG" —CLAY SCULPTURE BY MARILYN ANDERSON — NATIONAL INSTITUTE OF ART & DISABILITIES

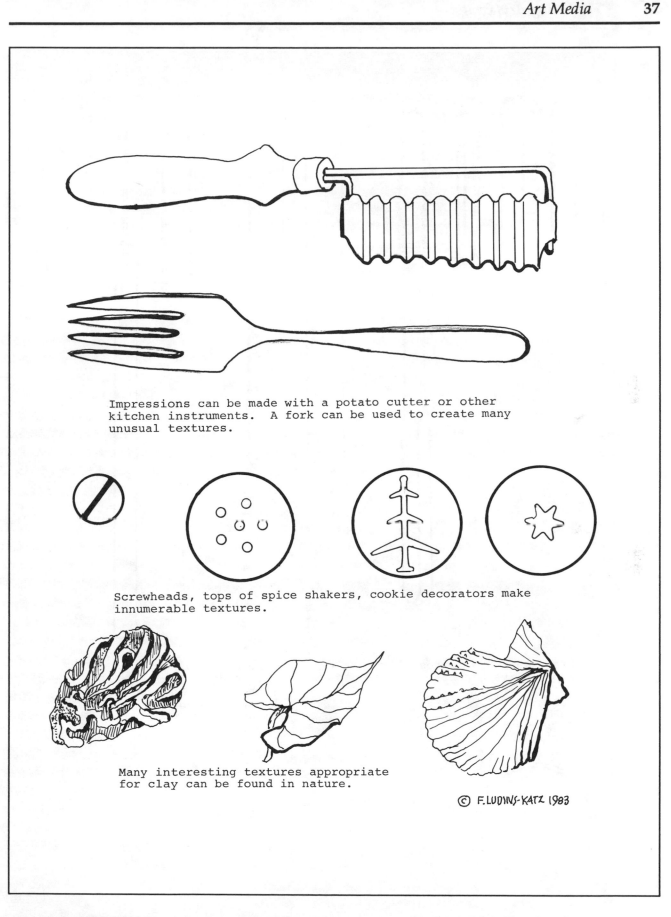

Impressions can be made with a potato cutter or other kitchen instruments. A fork can be used to create many unusual textures.

Screwheads, tops of spice shakers, cookie decorators make innumerable textures.

Many interesting textures appropriate for clay can be found in nature.

© F. LUDINS-KATZ 1983

CLAY TEXTURING

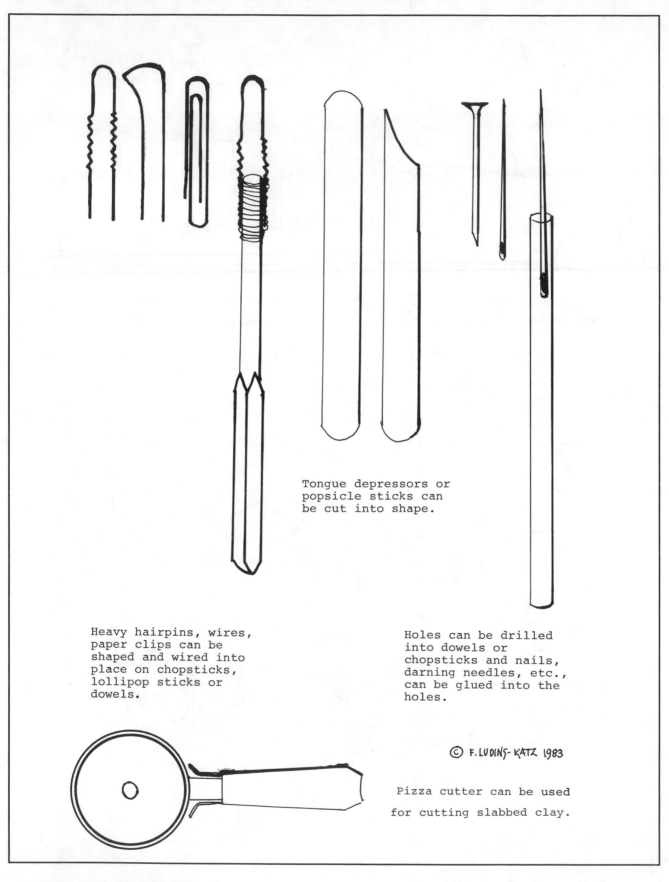

Tongue depressors or
popsicle sticks can
be cut into shape.

Heavy hairpins, wires,
paper clips can be
shaped and wired into
place on chopsticks,
lollipop sticks or
dowels.

Holes can be drilled
into dowels or
chopsticks and nails,
darning needles, etc.,
can be glued into the
holes.

© F. LUDINS-KATZ 1983

Pizza cutter can be used

for cutting slabbed clay.

HOMEMADE TOOLS FOR CLAY

Clay work which is not to be kept permanently can be thrown back into bins and recycled after photographs or slides of the work have been made. It is impossible to keep all the work. The first piece, significant changes, and outstanding pieces should be fired and perhaps glazed and kept for record or for exhibit. The best pieces should be placed in the Permanent Collection.

Glazes are used for waterproofing (cups, bowls, etc.) or for decoration. Glazes can be mixed from different chemicals or can be purchased in a prepared form. If time and space are important, it is less arduous to buy finished glazes than to mix them.

When handled correctly, work can be enhanced by glazing. Students usually like to see their work in color. However, in our experience, we have seen many beautiful ceramic pieces ruined by poor glazing. Not all pieces benefit from the glazing process and many are far more beautiful in the bisque stage (fired but not glazed). However, it must be the choice of the student whether to glaze or not to glaze.

All clay objects must be fired for permanency. This usually requires a kiln. The gas kilns are excellent but need special installation. It is very often easier and cheaper to install an electric kiln which uses 220 volts, though there are some smaller kilns which use 110 volts. Before installation, research should be done concerning the fumes from firing. Some fumes can be harmful and toxic in a small, closed area.

It is a good idea when purchasing a kiln not to buy one that is too small. This will limit the size of the pieces produced and may become extremely frustrating to both students and teachers. Sometimes it is wise to wait until one of the proper size can be purchased. During the interim, pieces can usually be fired in kilns at schools, art associations, artists' studios, etc.

Other interesting means of firing are pit firing and raku. This requires a good deal of research since many cities prohibit outdoor firing. If a beach or river bank is available this would be an excellent and inexpensive method to use.

In pit firing a hole is dug in the earth or sand. The completely dried clay objects are placed in the hole and covered with sawdust, leaves and manure, then fired for several hours. The most unusual and unexpected results occur. We have even seen this method of pit firing done in the yards of city museums. In raku firing a glazed piece of ceramic is placed in the pit. Both of these methods should be tried if possible.

Papier Mache Sculpture

Papier mache is an excellent material for those students who like to work in large three-dimensional forms. Clay is often difficult to handle when the forms become large.

We have had students who built armatures from coat hanger wires and strapping tape four to five feet high. The paper (newspaper or paper towels) can be made into a mush with paper hanger's paste and applied to the armature. Dry paper can be rolled tightly over the armature and glued or strapped into place with tape. The sculpture is usually finished by applying torn strips of paper dipped in paste. The finished work can be large rough masses or can be handled with great delicacy and detail. After the work is thoroughly dry the surface can be left as it is or finished by applying plaster of paris or gesso. Both of these will give an extremely smooth finish, especially after sanding. Textures can easily be added.

The finished work can be painted with tempera or acrylics. Decorations of wood, pebbles, feathers, or found objects can enhance the work. The whole can be covered with leather, fur, or material. There is no end to the possibilities that students encouraged to use their imagination can bring to this simple material.

Masks are a particularly excellent project for papier mache.

Wood and Stone Sculpture

Some students have a great desire to do both three-dimensional and relief carving. The concept of visualizing what will remain when sections of wood or stone are cut away is a difficult one. This can be a very frustrating experience. This method should be reserved for those who can understand the process and are capable of carrying it out. In addition, it is a difficult medium for severely disabled people since cutting away stone and wood takes strength many lack. Also, it may be dangerous for some people to handle sharp knives and chisels. However, most people can be trained to handle tools carefully and there are those with great physical strength. Candidates for this work must be assessed and supervised carefully. There is no reason why those who have a particular aptitude cannot do this most important form of sculpture.

Materials are wood, both hard and soft, soap stone, and alabaster. Tools consist of a variety of chisels, sculptors' mallets, sharp knives, different types and sizes of files, and many different types and gradations of sandpaper.

Dremel type electric tools can also be used. When using electric tools, masks must be worn at all times to prevent inhaling the particles that are sent into the air. This is especially important in the case of people with respiratory problems.

We have tried soap as a substitute for wood or stone, but have not found this a satisfactory experience. Just when everything is going well and the piece seems to be successfully on its way, a section of soap breaks off, leading to great disappointment.

We know of a group of blind people who work with chisels, files, and sandpaper in soft stone, creating excellent carvings of three-dimensional figures. For this particular group, it seems the answer to their special needs.

Sculpture with Found Objects (Assemblage)

One of the most satisfying and simple forms of sculpture is working with "found objects" and creating three-dimensional sculpture from them. These objects may be man-made materials such as cast-off machinery, plumbing parts, pattern-makers' wooden parts, parts of furniture, building materials, cardboard, plastic, meshes, and screws.

Another source of found objects is natural forms such as driftwood, feathers, shells, branches of trees, etc. These pieces can be assembled into an interesting sculptural whole and either glued, tied, or nailed together. The student learns to build, to assemble, to use nails and hammer, and finds a way of making disparate objects conform to his concept.

Having large boxes filled with these materials in the studio leads to imaginative sculptural pieces. Many times decorative accents are added using bits of metal, fibers, shells, stones, tiles, etc. Students can be trained to spot interesting materials and will often bring them from home, from their trips to beaches and parks, or even from city streets.

As an art experience, they become aware of the relationships of sizes, shapes, textures and colors. The finished assemblage can be painted or left in its natural colors, showing the patina of age and weather.

COLLAGE

Collage is the experience of adhering flat or three-dimensional materials or objects onto a flat surface such as wood or cardboard. Favorite two-dimensional materials are newspapers, fabrics, labels, sandpaper, and tissue paper. Three-dimensional materials consist of natural objects such as seeds, grasses, bark, pebbles, or man-made objects such as bolts, nuts, springs,

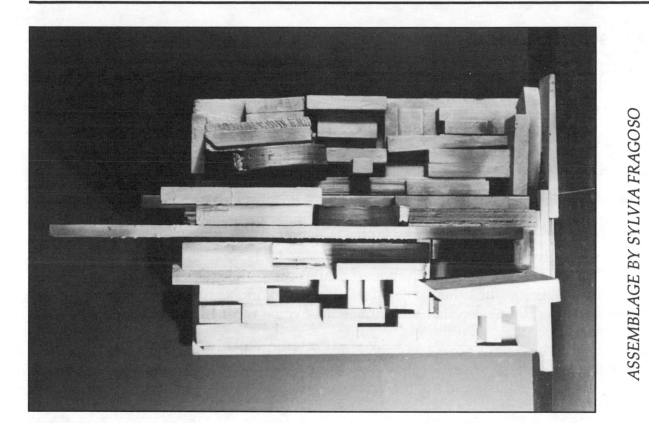

ASSEMBLAGE BY SYLVIA FRAGOSO

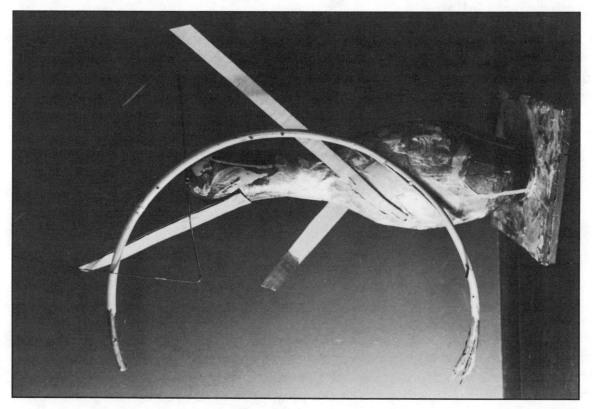

ASSEMBLAGE BY ANGELA CAMPBELL

or bits and pieces of machinery. This is an inexpensive and interesting art experience for all art students.

Although many objects in a collage may be three-dimensional, essentially the collage remains a flat two-dimensional work of art and not a three-dimensional sculptural form.

Many modern artists add collage to their paintings for textural effects. Picasso, Braque, Schwitters, and Burri are artists who made a great deal of use of this technique.

Paper Collage

In one type of collage all that is needed is a variety of textural papers which can be found in supermarket wrappings, oriental wrappings, magazines, wallpaper sample books, colored tissue paper, etc. A piece of cardboard on which to paste the material, a pair of scissors, and a bottle of paste or glue are the only other supplies needed.

Some students may wish to cut the papers while others prefer tearing them. Some enjoy superimposed images while others enjoy dealing with colors, textures, and shapes. Others prefer using colored tissues so that undertones may come through the transparencies and create unusual effects.

In setting up the collage table, it is a good idea to lay out different stimulating colors and textures in the center of the table. Cardboard or heavy paper should be positioned where each student is to sit. Glue or paste and a pair of scissors should be placed near each student or may be shared by two students.

We have observed many teachers place magazines in the center of a table, expecting students to rummage through them to find appropriate materials. This is an extremely poor method since the stimulation of seeing a variety of colors and textures does not present itself. The students spend much time looking at pictures but seldom look for color, shape and texture.

Three-Dimensional Collage

Another type of collage uses three-dimensional materials glued to a flat surface. Excellent materials are natural bark, seeds, twigs, feathers, weeds, small pebbles (rough and smooth). Other interesting materials are manufactured items such as washers, nuts, nails, plastics, beads, buttons, parts of watches, clocks, radios, etc. Many students find handling and arranging such objects very satisfying and can create a work of art that is aesthetically pleasing. Collage can also be combined with painting.

It is important for the students to discover the objects they wish to place in a collage. Before undertaking this project, it would be an excellent experience to go on a collecting trip to beaches, parks, or even a walk in the city streets.

PRINTMAKING

Making an image on a plate, inking the plate, sending the plate through a press, and seeing the image emerge on paper is an experience that should not be missed. If one watches the faces of students in anticipation of what will happen as the paper is pulled from the plate, the real significance of the event is apparent.

Usually we think of printmaking as a complicated process needing great skill and control. However, there are so many ways of improvising that a good teacher can make printing a relatively simple process. When one thinks of how much the students can gain by being exposed to the various stimulating aspects of the print process, it becomes essential that it should be included in the studio.

One of the big expenses in printmaking is the cost of a press. A good etching press is a decided advantage. The prints are more professional and the process of printing becomes much more exciting. However, good prints can be made without a press. It is advisable to hold off purchase of a press until a good one can be bought. Cheap presses are ineffectual, frustrating, and constantly break down.

Printers ink comes both in oil base and water base. We advise using the water based inks. Oil based inks provide health and fire hazards and are difficult to clean up.

Monoprints

Making a monoprint serves as a good introduction to the printing process. In the usual method printers ink is rolled onto a plate (metal or plastic). The ink is removed by cloth, a dauber, or pencil, wherever white is required. When the image on the plate is satisfactory, paper is placed on the plate and either sent through the press, rolled with a clean brayer or rubbed with a baren or spoon back. The paper is carefully separated from the plate and the image is born. This is a tremendous thrill, especially for those who have never seen a print made.

A monoprint can also be made by painting on a plate with tempera. Different colors can be painted on the same plate before printing or can be added with a second or third impression on the original print.

Only one good impression can be made from the inked plate. Hence the name, monoprint.

Printing with Different Shaped and Textured Blocks

Before attempting a wood or linoleum block it would be advisable to start with the very simple process of stamping or printing with blocks. Different shapes of wood such as circles, squares, and rectangles should be cut. The wood should be thick enough to grasp. Found objects such as washers, buttons, and coins can be glued to wooden dowels so they can be held. Even textured cardboard, wallpaper, and fibers can be used, as long as they are glued to a flat piece of wood thick enough to be held.

The students sit around a table with all these wondrous pieces in the center. Each student has a piece of paper in front of him. The object is to make a design, printing with these forms. The student inks or paints the object and stamps it on the paper. He continues using many different forms or perhaps one form. He may print in many colors or only one color.

This exercise makes the student understand the true meaning of printing.

Linoleum and Wood Blocks

Linoleum and wood block prints are made by cutting away all surfaces of the block which are to remain white after printing. The remaining surfaces which are not cut away will be inked and printed. After applying printer's ink (black or colored ink), the block can be printed on paper or cloth with a printing press or by pressure from a spoon, baren, or brayer.

Many interesting effects can be obtained by cutting into different textured and weathered woods. The Japanese take special advantage of the wood. They are masters of the wood block.

Multi-colored block prints may be made by using a different block for each different color. Each block is printed separately on the same sheet of paper or cloth. Each block must be exactly aligned with the other blocks. This is a precise process and should not be undertaken with students who have a low frustration level. However, if freedom of expression is more

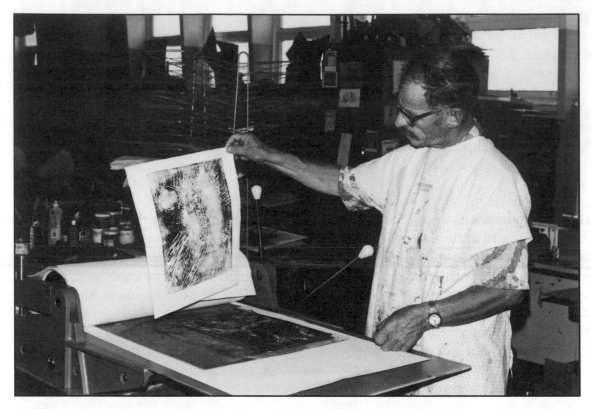

BEVERLY TRIEBER MAKING A MONOPRINT ON THE PRESS

BLOCK PRINT WITH DIFFERENT SHAPED AND TEXTURED
WOOD PIECES - JAMES BOUTELL

important than exactness, many beautiful effects can be gotten when colors overlay each other.

Relief Block Print

A pattern is built up from various materials glued onto a thin piece of wood or heavy cardboard. Various shapes may be cut from cardboard, rubber, or fiber mats having different textures. Shapes may be natural or man-made objects. Found objects are excellent. The textures and shapes of crumpled metal, thin gears, and washers can be built into most interesting abstract designs when glued to the background.

The paper is dampened. The block is inked with a brayer and is either sent through the press or rubbed by hand. Only the raised inked surfaces are printed. Very often part of the design is embossed or raised.

As a precaution, the objects must not be too high and they should be kept to about the same height whenever possible. When the objects are too different in height, printing becomes difficult. When objects are too high, the paper tears and the press may be damaged.

Collagraph

Collagraph takes its name from collage. Various objects and shapes are glued onto a flat background precisely as in the relief block print. The difference between the two processes is that only the recessed areas are printed. The raised surfaces are wiped clean. When the block is printed on damp paper only the inked background is printed and the resultant print is embossed due to pressure on the paper.

Precaution: the objects must not be too high nor may they be of too great variety in thickness, as this may tear the paper or may damage the press. It is best to postpone this type of printing until a press is purchased since it is very difficult to print collagraphs by hand.

Engraving

The image that one wishes to obtain can be scratched on a plate of plastic or soft metal or even pressed into heavy non-absorbent paper. Tools are either professional, such as gravers or burins, or can be improvised, using dental tools, darning needles fixed into wooden dowels for handles, or sharpened awls. An electric tool similar to a Dremel tool is excellent. If used, a mask must be worn to prevent inhaling the particles of metal or plastic.

The plate is inked and wiped so that only the incised lines contain the ink. When printed, the wider the line the darker the print. A paper, preferably damp, is placed on the plate and sent through the press. Although the image may not be as clear, the print may be made by rubbing with a baren or a spoon so that all the ink from the incised lines is transferred to the paper.

Etching

Since etching requires the use of acids, it is not advisable to make this type of print in the Art Studio.

Lithography

Lithography is a complicated process and usually should be avoided in the Art Studio.

Silk Screen (Serigraph)

Silk screen is essentially a stencil process. A very fine piece of silk or voile is stretched and nailed tautly on a frame or canvas stretcher about two inches high. The artist blocks out the screen where he does not wish color to appear, using a paper stencil or film tusche-washout method. The paper or cloth to be printed is laid under the screen. The color is then poured onto one side of the frame and spread with a rubber squeegee. The image appears on the paper below. To make prints of more than one color, usually a separate screen is used for each color. Each separate color must be superimposed (registered) carefully. This may be too challenging for many students. However, the one-color silk screen is a relatively simple process and is a very stimulating experience. To vary the effect, different colors can be poured in the frame, giving varied colors with just one screen.

This fine art process is often used to make posters, as well as images on tee shirts, table cloths, banners, and towels.

MOSAIC

A mosaic is made by adhering small pieces (tesserae) of tile, stone, glass, shell, or pottery to a wood, masonite, or heavy cardboard backing. Usually the tesserae are glued on a flat surface, but mosaics can be glued on three-dimensional forms and figures. Beniamino Bufano's sculpture is a good example.

Many students delight in working with these bits of three-dimensional color and can make beautiful mosaics. Some who have difficulty in handling paints find these pieces easier to manipulate. It is important that mosaics should only be done when the student finds it a stimulating experience. As soon as it becomes repetitive it is time to stop and to continue another day.

This is an extremely inexpensive project, since discontinued tile can be obtained free at most big hardware or tile shops. The students delight in breaking up the tiles with a hammer. To do so, place the tiles in a paper bag so that pieces will not fly. A tile cutter is inexpensive and students can be taught to use this tool. Bits of wood and shells can be picked up on the beaches. Colored stones and broken crockery can be obtained without cost.

After the mosaic is completed it can be framed and grouted. However, this is not essential.

Creating a mosaic teaches discrimination in the use of color and texture in design. It is an extremely interesting experience when a group of students work together on a very large mosaic, each creating a different section. This can be a wall hanging, a floor, or a totem pole. The beauty of the completed mosaic, especially when the sun shines on these bits of colored glass and interesting textures of shells and pebbles, gives the students delight in their accomplishment.

FIBER ART

Many wonderful experiences can be had in working with fiber. Fiber includes threads of any thickness or material. Among these are wools, silks, hemp, cords, straw, cottons, and the vast number of new synthetic fibers. Fibers can be woven, glued onto cardboard or wood, used as decorations on masks and sculpture. Fibers can be used by themselves or in conjunction with clay, wood, beads, shells, rocks, screws, nuts, bolts, and other hardware.

MAKING A MOSAIC

MOSAIC BY LESLIE SYLVESTER

Weaving

Weaving can be made very simple by using frames or stretcher bars. Nails driven into opposite ends of the frame will hold the warp. Students can learn the process of working over one thread and under the next thread, or of going over or under more than one thread at a time. Buttons, beads, shells, metal washers can easily be added to the weaving to enhance its quality.

The delight will come from the color and texture of the different fibers and the resultant woven piece. Even though there are many students who may find it hard to follow these directions, mistakes will not spoil the effect of a beautifully colored and textured weaving.

For those more advanced, large looms can be made or purchased. There are many Art Centers for people with disabilities (especially in Scandinavia) which specialize in this form of art. Place mats, belts, woven yardage produced in these Art Centers are much in demand.

Fiber Sculpture

Many exciting pieces of modern sculpture are completely made of fiber. The cords or wools are manipulated into different shapes and tied or glued together into recognizable or abstract forms.

Students can work by themselves or in groups to produce a piece of sculpture. They will learn to discriminate colors, textures, and shapes. They will learn what can be done and what cannot be done. Each individual is so different that teachers will find those who may not enjoy sculpture in clay or wood may enjoy sculpture in fiber.

Fiber Used in Sculpture, Masks, Assemblage, Collage

Very often students will use fiber to enhance a piece of sculpture by adding the color and texture of the fiber. This can be used with abstract sculpture and on sculpture of the human form. Masks gain much decorative value by using fiber as hair or gluing fiber on other parts of the mask for emphasis.

Assemblage and collage may use fiber as their main materials or fiber can be used as decorative accents.

Gluing Fiber on Cardboard or Wood

An excellent fiber project is having students glue wools of various colors and thicknesses on wood, masonite, or cardboard, after making a design. The Huichol Indians of Mexico specialize in this form of art. There is no limitation as to the simplicity or complexity with which this project can be handled.

Embroidery and Stitchery

Many students delight in simple embroidery. Designs must always be their own. They will gain much from selecting colors and textures. Many become extremely proficient in this art. Large tapestries have been created for public buildings by disabled students working individually or in teams. An example is the tapestries created by mentally retarded persons in the studios of Le Fil D'Ariane, Quebec, Canada. Here each student made his own design and after much practice embroidered it in a simple stitch. The designs were then sewn together to form a huge tapestry which hangs in a government building.

This chapter does not fully describe the different media nor does it describe the different ways a studio can be set up for working with disabled people. It is rather a presentation of materials and methods we have found comfortable and appropriate. Each teacher must improvise methods and seek materials that best suit the needs of his students and take advantage of his own expertise. This is indeed a challenge.

8 Art Experimentation

The importance of art experimentation is in learning what you can do with colors, shapes, textures, lines, materials and tools and what you cannot do, of seeing for yourself how images and shapes will develop, will slide away, and will take shape again. Subject matter is important when it stimulates visual imagery. The real thrill is in learning through experiencing a totally new way of expression.

A student should take his time and get as much as he can from each experience. It can be disastrous if a student is pushed by the teacher to try new experiments before he is ready to give up the old accustomed ways. The student alone will know when he is ready and willing to take on new and challenging experiences.

Experimentation with Different Materials and Methods

The student experiments with different colors, intensities, and values of paint, crayon and chalk on different textures, shapes and colors of paper, metal, cloth, and board. He experiments with light and dark relationships. The student also uses different brushes—soft and hard, thick and thin.

The student experiments with different drawing materials. He tries hard pencils, soft pencils. He works with charcoal, conte crayon, lithographic crayon, pens and ink and felt pens. All of these experiences help to build up a "feel" of what can be done, the different ways each drawing material works and its effect on different surfaces. He learns how to get special effects.

The student experiments with different textures. In any visual art experience textures play an important role. The textures of papers—the smooth slick surfaces of coated paper, the roughness of some water color paper, the textural differences in pieces of Japanese paper—all play a big role in the kind of stimulation they invoke and in the finished result. A clay sculpture appears very different when it is silky smooth or woolly rough. The textural effects of different paints, thin coats or heavy layers, are the result of the artist's concept.

Experimentation with found objects such as nails, wires, corrugated cardboard, rough weathered wood, shells and pebbles should be engaged in by the students.

The student works with clay. He rolls, coils, flattens, pinches, builds up, destroys, and starts again. He learns to put shapes together, to cut them apart, to make them adhere. He learns to decorate by carving, incising, by adding. He uses different tools and objects to create different textures. He learns the quality of clay and what he can do and what he cannot do. After the work is dry and fired, he learns to apply glaze.

The student experiments with papier mache. He learns how to mix paper and paste, to build with strips, to build with paper pulp, to create smooth and rough textures. He learns how to build armatures, how to apply the paper to the armatures. After the work is dry he learns to paint the papier mache and to decorate it with leather, feathers, stones, etc.

The student experiments with collage. He learns to discriminate light and dark, bright and dull colors. He works with textures. He learns to build one texture and color upon the other or to place them side by side. Shapes emerge and shapes disappear. He cuts and tears and creates rough edges and smooth edges. He uses transparencies and opaque colors. He works with decorative feathers, buttons, beads, bits of metal, shiny textures, dull textures. He learns the stimulation of tactile experience.

The student experiments with assemblage. He learns to build, to assemble tubes, wood, metal parts. He uses a hammer and nails and finds ways of making disparate objects conform in concept. He decorates and finds objects that please him in texture, shape and color. He paints the objects where he wishes. He leaves others as he finds them, enjoying the patina of age and weather.

The student experiments with printing by cutting, by blocking out, by adding to areas. He has the experience of printing and stamping, of seeing the image appear. He has the thrill of making exact duplicates of his work and seeing what happens to the same image when he uses different colors, papers and textures.

Experimentation with Abstract Art

Students enjoy creating with colors and shapes, dark and light. What they create need not resemble or be a reproduction of a real object. Many shapes are satisfying in themselves. A circle need not be a head nor a cylinder a tree trunk. So often teachers ask, "What are you making?" and a student will answer in amazement, "Colors." A wise teacher allows each student to follow his own inclinations.

Many students are abstractionists just as many artists are. They have no desire to create "real" things. These students should be allowed to do what they most enjoy.

Many museum visitors are more moved by color abstractions than by a most glorious painting of fields of flowers. Tremendous abstractions of stone and steel can be more powerful than the sculpture of a Greek god. Art is in the eye of the creator and man must respect the vision of the artist.

Experimentation with Objects and Groups in the Studio

Students should be encouraged to draw, paint, and sculpt the objects they see about them in the studio such as chairs, cabinets, plants, pipes, wall divisions, etc. They learn much through observation and setting down their ideas. They can also combine the objects in a realistic or imaginative way.

It is an excellent idea to have different studio setups. Sometimes flowers can be arranged to stimulate desire to draw and paint. Bottles of all sizes and colors can be arranged dramatically so that students become interested in drawing or painting the various shapes. An old art school setup is a large platter containing fruit against a cloth with a small vase in front. But there are many different setups that can be done with unusual or junk objects as well. Tools can be extremely interesting in shape, color, and variety of sizes and textures.

Experiments with Portraits

Students are interested in themselves. Imaginary or reflected images of themselves in mirrors are a constant source of fun. Mirrors can be set up by making a simple stand to hold them. Students observe themselves and paint themselves realistically, abstractly, or decoratively.

Portraits are interesting adventures in art. For variety a student or a group of students can pose for the rest of the class. Sometimes volunteers or teachers may do the posing. A group portrait of the class can be made with each student contributing.

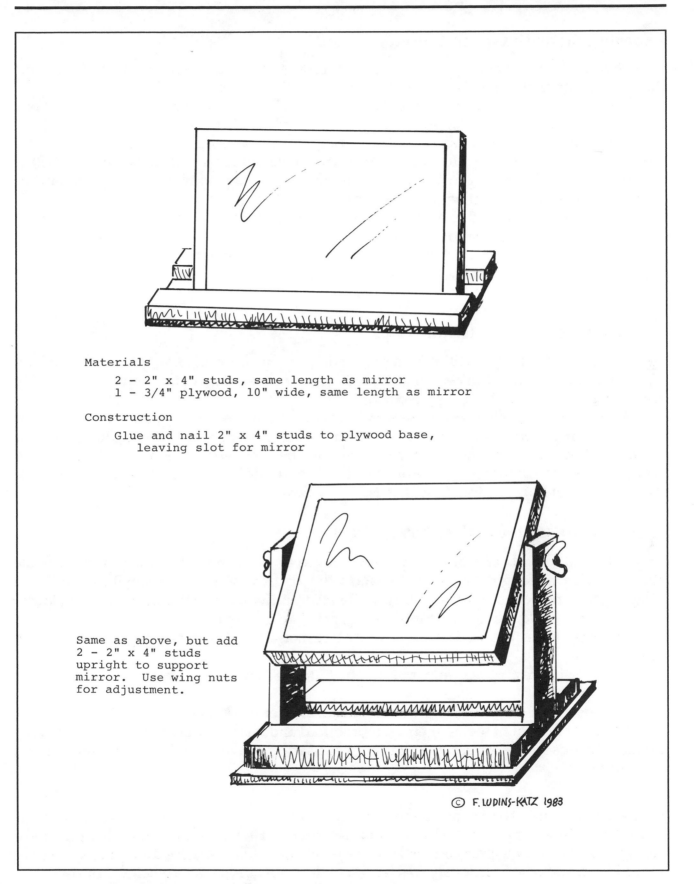

Materials

    2 – 2" x 4" studs, same length as mirror
    1 – 3/4" plywood, 10" wide, same length as mirror

Construction

    Glue and nail 2" x 4" studs to plywood base,
       leaving slot for mirror

Same as above, but add
2 – 2" x 4" studs
upright to support
mirror. Use wing nuts
for adjustment.

© F. LUDINS-KATZ 1983

MIRRORS FOR SELF-PORTRAITS

Experiments with Group Projects

Groups of students can work together on a single project. It draws the group together and helps the individuals communicate with each other and with the teacher.

One of the great pitfalls to be avoided in group projects is having the teacher or one student design the whole and all the other students simply fill in the shapes with colors, objects, or fibers. This applies to murals, sculpture projects, tapestries, and mosaics. It may be a wonderfully creative project for the leader but the other students will continue in a lifelong pattern of dependency. A good teacher can easily invent ways in which each person in the group can perform at a high level, using his own creativity and originality.

Murals can be done either in the studio or outdoors. Murals on designated fences or walls are a real fun project. The students interact with the community—a definite asset to both.

Sculpture projects in which each student contributes one building or one figure are other fun events. Abstract work in wood, where all the parts are fitted together to make one great whole, is another excellent way to unify the group.

Experiments with Sketching Trips

Groups visit interesting localities both near and far. They take sketching material with them and make sketches for studio work. When they return they may paint, draw, or sculpt the scenes or objects which have inspired them.

Sometimes these visits result in abstract drawings, paintings, or sculpture such as a blue and green composition inspired by the water or a painting with large swinging lines inspired by the motion of a ferris wheel. Other students may become interested in a single object and make a realistic sculpture of a horse or a vendor's stand. At other times students create whole compositions of horse racing, flower beds, or landscape.

Experiments with Specific Assignments

Very often individuals or groups can be encouraged to work on a specific assignment. Some students enjoy making their own books and will work for weeks perfecting illustrations on each page. Some books will tell a story while other individuals prefer to have much looser themes. These books can be done in drawing, painting, or prints.

At other times the students will work together, each doing one page for a book or calendar.

Another interesting assignment is to illustrate the Newsletter for the Art Center or for another agency.

Posters can be made both for the Art Center and for other agencies.

Students delight in seeing their art reproduced and it is an excellent way for the agency to make friends in the community. It is not necessary that every student take part in all art assignments.

Each student should have exposure to as many experiences as he is capable of absorbing. He should be able to experiment with this vast assortment. He will in time find the art he most enjoys and will become proficient in his chosen field or fields. All these different experiences should be introduced judiciously so the student does not become overwhelmed or confused. Many teachers introduce new ideas only when interest and experimentation wane. In this way teachers once again are able to arouse excitement and the spirit of new adventure.

9 Adventures in Art

Think of each new art experience as an art adventure. An adventure need not involve going anywhere but may be an adventure of using new materials or using familiar materials in a new way. An adventure may be a way of seeing the world around you or it may be a new idea that you act upon in your art.

In a classroom, a teacher must make presentations that are exciting and imaginative in order to arouse the enthusiasm of the students. Teachers must be well prepared and must present each adventure after much thought. The following are some issues to be considered:

o The benefits to each student and to the group.
o Materials to be used.
o Difficulties that may arise due to disabilities and how to surmount them.
o The process of making each adventure stimulating to the student's imagination and creativity.
o Culmination in a finished product pleasing to the student.
o Places where the end results may be shown, even if only in the studio, so the student may feel achievement and self-worth.

These adventures may take only one day or they may be of prolonged duration. It has been our experience that some students after a stimulating experience will work on their own for long periods and will wish to repeat this experience many times. For example, they may wish to make four or five different masks or four or five collages. If interest wanes, the project should be put away and reintroduced at a later date. Following are a few adventures which we have found successful.

Sketching Trips to Museums, Zoos, Botanical Gardens, Aquariums, Beaches, etc.

This adventure depends on many factors, among them the closeness of the Art Center to the destination, the transportation, the mobility of the group, the expense, etc.

Before going, the teacher should be acquainted with the destination. It is a good idea to discuss the trip with the students who are going and to emphasize what they will be seeing and what will be expected of them. The excitement of such an adventure is contagious.

Preparations must be made by the staff before such an adventure. Art materials must be gathered together for each student. Among them are sketch pads (loose paper is not a good idea, since it adds to confusion and is difficult to work on), drawing materials for each student, such as pencils, felt pens, crayons, etc. Materials difficult to use or bulky materials should not be considered. It would be most advisable for each student to have a cloth bag with handles with his name on it. The pad and drawing materials should be placed inside. If the student brings a brown bag lunch, he should place it in the cloth bag so that he has one bag to carry.

After the students arrive back in the studio, they will be able to translate these sketches into drawings, paintings, prints, collages, or any other type of finished work. The stimulation that the adventure provides can be translated into weeks of work.

To illustrate, we will consider an adventure that the students of the Art Center were involved in. A new park called "Africa USA" was established in Vallejo, California. There was much publicity; the students had heard of the park and were anxious to go. This park is about 20 miles from the Art Center. The first step was to find out the practicality since there was no public transportation available. Two months in advance transportation was arranged with a company whose charitable contribution is taking nonprofit organizations on trips.

As the time for the trip drew near, the teachers began to talk with the students about Africa USA. The students knew they would see strange animals, that dolphins and whales would perform. There was no problem in stimulating their desire to go.

A week before the trip one of the teachers went to Africa USA to see the layout, the problems that might arise, and to talk to the site staff. Bags were made from heavy cloth by volunteers since the Center could not afford the price of commercial ones. Cheap drawing pads for each student were contributed by a printer. Simple drawing materials—pencils, crayons, felt pens—were gathered and placed in each student's bag.

The day before the adventure, the students were told exactly what was expected of them: adult behavior, staying with the group, drawings of anything that interested them, including the animals, the fish, trees, people, buildings, or abstract patterns. Students were told that they would make these sketches into paintings, sculpture, or prints at the Art Center.

On the great day the bus was filled with enthusiastic students, well prepared teachers, and volunteers. One staff person was responsible for no more than five students. It was decided that all would buy and eat lunch together in one of the concessions.

On arrival, after taking time to investigate the surroundings, the students took out their pads and drew. How differently each one worked!

There were scrappy little drawings of a few lines. There were many finished pages of drawings, some sophisticated, some primitive. Some tried to reproduce exactly what they saw, while others simply made designs. The teachers encouraged each student to work in whatever way the student was capable of and enjoyed. When the day was ended much material for future use was both in the mind and on the paper of each student.

The day after the trip was devoted to working on the material the students had gathered. Fish, zebras, giraffes came alive on paper.

Making of Masks

The making of a mask can be a marvelous adventure. So many new experiences come together to make a unified whole. There is manipulation with form, with color, with texture, and with design.

Masks have a universal appeal. Throughout civilization we find the mask—Egypt, Africa, Greece, Rome, Japan, Alaska, New Guinea, etc. All modern countries use the mask in one form or another. Among the types of masks are dance masks, death masks, ritual masks, decorative masks, holiday masks, etc.

In a lesson on mask making, even the most disabled person can gain much by a combination of discussion and seeing the marvelous and imaginative forms of masks. Real masks can be brought into the studio. Slides can be shown. Students can see complete art books on masks and pictures can be clipped from such magazines as *National Geographic*.

The whole group becomes excited if students are given the opportunity to try on three-dimensional masks which can be borrowed from personal collections, stores, or museums.

After the introduction, the fun really begins. Masks can be made from paper bags, papier mache, leather, cloth, or can be carved from wood. They can be painted with tempera or

PHOTO OF MASK FORM

DECORATED MASK

acrylics, and trimmed with buttons, feathers, wool, or found objects.

A book can be written about making masks. However, we will restrict ourselves to one simple process, hoping all teachers will invent their own techniques, depending on their resources and the ability of their students.

A very simple way of making a mask is by using a styrofoam base generally used as a wig stand. The form is cut lengthwise, to produce two heads, each flat on one side. These can be purchased cheaply in second hand stores, such as the Salvation Army or Goodwill stores. They can be used indefinitely. This form enables the student to make a good-sized mask which he can place over his face. As the styrofoam has no features, the student will use his imagination in building up the form he wishes.

Place a plastic sheet over the form so that the mask will easily slip from the styrofoam form when dry. Place strips of newspaper dipped in paperhanger's paste across the form (be sure to use the paste that contains no arsenic). Criss-cross the paper, using about five layers. These can be easily distinguished by using different colored newspapers.

Now build ears, eyes, nose, mouth, either by using paper pulp (mashed paper) or by building these forms with strips. Encourage imagination. Show that surfaces can protrude, that forms can go in and forms can be built up. Don't expect each student to understand these concepts the first time. Eventually they will learn.

Be careful that the student is not pushed beyond his understanding. Leave the student to work out his own ideas. The teacher is there to guide and encourage but not to make demands or to work on the student's mask. Sometimes, for lower functioning students, just applying the paper strips with paste and later painting the mask is a great experience.

After the mask is finished and dried, it is easily removed from the styrofoam base. It can be painted in tempera or acrylic. Water color or oils are not recommended. The painting can be extremely imaginative, using different colors and different textural effects.

Now comes the trimming. Feathers, beads, buttons, and wools can be glued onto the base. Watch a class go to a table filled with odds and ends with exciting colors, shapes, and textures of all sorts. Watch the students rummage through this wonderful assortment, picking out those things they wish to use for decorating their masks. Buttons and beads become eyes; shells become teeth; wool becomes mustaches, hair, eyebrows, and decorations on the face; feathers become headdresses, necklaces, earrings; and so it goes. There is no limit to what the imagination can dream up.

Printmaking with Found Objects

Printing is a wonderful adventure. To see images appear on paper without drawing or painting is an exciting experience. Printmaking takes many forms. Printing can be done on paper, on cloth, on wallpaper, and may be combined with other types of painting. The principle is the same in all printing. A block is inked and then placed upon and pressed onto another surface. A description of many types of prints can be found in the previous chapter. For this adventure, we will use one of the simplest types of printmaking, one that all students will be able to do and will enjoy.

Teachers and students gather materials for printing. These must be flat on one side so they can be inked. They gather different shapes, sizes, and textures of wood, small flat metal objects such as washers, gaskets, interestingly textured plastic pieces, sections of wooden molding from frames. Pieces should be large enough to be held and inked easily, and small enough to be printed on a sheet of paper.

The only other equipment needed are ink rollers, tubes of water-based printers ink (tempera and brushes may be substituted), and small pieces of plexiglass, 12" x 12". Each roller should be placed next to a piece of plexiglass with one color of printers ink on it. Paper should be placed before each student. The found objects should be in the middle of the table where all students can reach them.

Now the fun begins! Each student rolls ink on one of the objects, which is now called a block. He stamps the block on the paper. He picks up a second block and rolls either the same color or a different color on it, and again stamps it on the paper. When the process is complete the whole paper may be stamped (or printed) with many shapes, colors, and textures overlapping one another, or the whole paper may be printed in just one color and one shape stamped in many different ways. There is no end to the variety of this type of print process. It can be used as a picture when printed on paper, as a textile when printed on cloth, or can be used in combination with paintings in acrylic, water colors, tempera, or can be used to enhance sculptural forms.

Almost all students can understand the idea of inking a small object and turning it over so that the print (impression) can be made. But for those few low-functioning students who do not understand the process, one can attach a dowel to the back of the object by drilling a hole and gluing it. The student then has no trouble inking the object and no choice but to hold the dowel and turn the inked side down on the paper. The joy of this experience is no less great and eventually these students learn to use a block without the dowel.

This type of printmaking has many benefits both to the individual and to the group:

o   A student must select shapes that are interesting to him.
o   The shapes must be printed in an interesting order.
o   Shapes can overlap and be combined, making new shapes.
o   Background, or negative space, must be considered as part of the whole picture or design.

The students come to realize that overprinting with two colors produces a third color. Two or more colors must be judged in terms of how they appear when juxtaposed. Students can combine printing with their paintings, and achieve rich and varied textural effects.

A group of students can work together, learning to share blocks and colors, printing on one paper. The whole group takes pride in the finished product.

Sculpture with Found Objects (Assemblage)

This is a fantastic experience which can be carried out in many ways. One very interesting way is to have students and teacher bring objects they would like to work with to the Art Center. We have seen parts of furniture (table legs, straw backs of chairs, decorative motifs such as curleycues and lions' heads) brought in, with the students getting excited about what can be done with them. Students who attend sheltered workshops have brought pieces of discarded packaging, stamped-out circles, and the like. Pattern makers have donated wonderful wooden shapes. Framers save their odds and ends of moldings—all bright and golden. Trips to the seashore provide weatherbeaten wood, shells, delightfully colored stones and pebbles, feathers, etc. All sorts of rope, bits of discarded machinery, bicycle parts are often brought in by the students who have had experience with this type of sculpture.

When the project begins, how interesting it is to watch the students make choices, picking up an object, discarding it in favor of another. The kind of stimulation and energy this kind of approach brings is a joy to the teacher. The stimulation of shapes, colors, and textures is already there. The challenge is to find means of nailing, gluing and tying together these disparate objects into a finished whole. You need only think of Louise Nevelson's work to understand the possibilities. We have seen the whole room with groups of students on the floor or working on tables, trying to assemble these objects, keeping some, discarding others, manipulating pieces in different positions.

The advantages of such a project are great. The students learn to share the materials. They take great pride in bringing in materials that can be used by themselves or others. They must learn to make decisions, very often difficult ones. They must learn to arrange and put together disparate objects. They must learn that their ideas will not work unless there is a way of actually putting the pieces together so they hold. When the assemblage is finally finished and is painted or sprayed, how very beautiful it looks on a stand in the studio or gallery.

Making a Group Portrait Mural

It is of great interest to look into a mirror, examine one's face, and draw oneself. Many projects can be built on this universal interest. One interesting method which uses each person's skill is making a mural of the whole group.

A mirror is made for each member. Each student is told to examine his eyes, nose, mouth, shape of his face, color and texture of his hair. Each one is then given a sheet of paper about 18" x 24" and told to paint his head and shoulders. No parameters are set as to color or style. The size of the head is limited by the sheet of paper. When the student finishes a satisfactory painting (he may make three or four), he cuts out his painted head and shoulders from the finished painting. A large sheet of wrapping paper or butcher paper, about 10 feet long, is tacked to the wall of the studio. As each student cuts out his self-portrait, he pins or tapes it to the background at whatever place he wishes. Rearranging their placement is easy, since the heads are not attached permanently.

When all the heads are satisfactorily placed, they are glued to the background paper. A group of students may then be chosen by the group to paint in a suitable background. You may not have a masterpiece at the end but all the students will have contributed and will enthusiastically point out their self-portrait to each other and to visitors.

It is amazing to realize how people see themselves. A black student may paint himself white, or a white student may paint himself blue. Long-haired students may see themselves with short curls. There is no end to the different colors of eyes! An interesting insight for the teacher is discovering who the student wishes to be next to on the mural. During this whole process, teachers learn much about the individual—his feelings about himself and his relationship to the group.

Other Art Adventures

Following is a list of art adventures that enthusiastic, imaginative, and knowledgeable art teachers can share with a class, a small group, or an individual. Some of these adventures may be real while others may be completely imaginary. All should result in a heightened awareness of the world and the possibilities of using these adventures to create a work of art.

Sketching Adventures

Zoos, beaches, amusement parks, botanical gardens, neighborhood parks, historical museums and places, art museums, street scenes, basements of buildings where machinery is working, etc. These trips should be taken with a sketch book in hand. The results may be realistic,

GROUP PORTRAIT - MURAL (SECTION)

designed, or abstract. They can be quick sketches or finished drawings. These adventures usually lead to class projects, using these experiences as a means of broadening horizons and seeing familiar objects in a new way.

Collecting Adventures

Beaches, lakes, mountains, walking down a street, going to cabinet maker shops, frame shops, printers, garage sales. These trips should always be undertaken with the permission of the person in charge of the premises to be visited. The teacher should give explicit directions as to what the student is expected to collect and what will be done with the materials. It is a good idea for each student to take a bag when he is on a collecting trip. Upon return from such trips, each student may work with the pieces he has collected or the collections can be shared by the group as a whole.

Adventures in the Studio

Sketching real objects such as chairs, tables, cabinets, stoves, sinks, etc. Painting from studio setups such as various arrangements of jars, dishes, and cloth. Painting or printmaking of flowers, leaves, and plants. Painting, printmaking, or sculpture from imagination, either realistic or abstract. Sculpting, drawing, and painting of staff and fellow students. Weaving abstract designs. And many others.

Adventures of the Imagination

Many artists use mental imagery in their work; Marc Chagall and Henri Rousseau are notable examples. Fantasy can be stimulated by showing movies, reading stories, going to the theater, watching a dance performance, hearing music, visiting a planetarium, etc. There is absolutely no end to the types of art projects that can be stimulated by such adventures. Feelings and moods can be expressed more easily after these types of experiences. In their art work students may go on a trip to the moon, or they may sail on a silver ocean, or they may find themselves surrounded by flowers. Others perhaps may be released to allow wondrous colors to float on their canvas.

The student should be encouraged to work in his own individual style, allowed to choose the materials and media which he enjoys. However, the teacher should encourage adventures into new ways of using the art media, of trying new media, new subject matter, and of experimenting.

To sum up this chapter, art is a challenge which may be expressed in never ending ways. It is up to the teacher to lead the student on a voyage of adventure and discovery.

10 Visits, Visiting Artists, and Art Events

From the very beginning, visits and trips to interesting art-related places should be incorporated into the program of the Art Center. Such trips add much to the enrichment of art experiences and expose people to a much wider range of stimulation than can be provided within the Art Center.

Visits to Artists' Studios

One of the most stimulating and exciting experiences for students is to visit a "real live artist" in his own studio. Many famous and important artists as well as unrecognized ones will gladly share their experiences and art work with a group of interested disabled persons. The students realize that art is a "real profession" and that "normal people" work in this field. Many artists use different and unorthodox materials and methods. Seeing such work opens the mind to hitherto undreamed of possibilities. To see the finished art, to be surrounded by work in all stages of progress, and to feel the dedication of the artist to his work is exciting to all of us.

Each visit should be limited to only a few students. If different groups are taken to visit different studios eventually all the students will be exposed to the experience. In selecting the students careful choices should be made. If a student works in a particular medium he probably will have most to gain from watching an artist work in this medium. For example, if a trip is planned to a water color artist's studio, the student most interested in water colors should be given preference. He would have the opportunity to see a variety of methods of using water colors—opaque and transparent, washes and layering of paint, the different textures of paper, painting on stretched or unstretched paper, the different sizes, shapes and types of brushes—and of seeing finished water color paintings. This visit adds a whole new dimension to the experience of the student. It is often surprising to their teachers how much the students understand, how perceptive their questions are, and how much they absorb even during a short visit.

Artists' Visits to the Art Center

The Center can designate certain days for artists to come to the Center to teach or take part in the activities. This is particularly appropriate if students have made a previous visit to the artist's studio and have established a bond of friendship and understanding with the artist.

The visiting artist has his choice of ways in which to work with the students. He may choose to work with only a few or with a larger group. He may wish to spend a full day or only a few hours. He may ask the Center to have certain supplies or he may bring whatever is needed with him. He may be the master teacher or he may prefer to work in a much less formal manner. He may wish to become just another student, another member of the studio. All these approaches are of inestimable value in making the Art Center a vital force in the art community.

Visits to Museums

An experience that should not be missed by anyone, especially art students, is visiting museums. They should have opportunities to see the greatest art of all ages and of all cultures. The museum is a constant source of visual delight, inspiration, and ideas.

Students should be taken in small groups with teachers, docents, or volunteers who are knowledgeable and can answer questions. Students should be encouraged to visit only a small portion of the museum on a single occasion. They should be given every opportunity to look, to study, to discuss, and to ask questions. In time, with visits to different areas, much of what is on display in the museum will be seen and absorbed by each person. There is nothing more frustrating for a teacher or guide than to herd a group of handicapped people through the museum with all other visitors staring. We have witnessed such insensitive behavior.

Visits to Galleries

Gallery visiting is a unique experience. There is something about the environment which makes art "important." Not only is the work of recognized artists shown, but many galleries will exhibit off-beat and experimental work before a museum finds this kind of art acceptable. Again, only a few students should go at a time, accompanied by a teacher or a volunteer who can answer questions and discuss significant aspects of the exhibit. Galleries are small and not taxing to people with limited emotional and physical capacity.

Visits to Exciting Art Happenings

Sometimes an Art Center is lucky enough to be near an exciting art event and the students should have the opportunity to either become part of such an event or to witness it. For example, an artist may build earth works. The students could see this in process and in its completed form. Another example is the work of Christo: his "Running Fence" or his "Valley Curtain." All students, wherever possible, should see such innovative expressions of art.

Visits to Open Studios

Many artists have open studios for the public once a year. This is especially true of artists who work in a cooperative setting. This may include the studios of potters, painters, sculptors, printmakers, glassblowers, weavers, etc. It is a real education to go from one studio to another and see the great variation of art work and method of execution. Often the artists put on demonstrations of their techniques.

Certainly the students of the Art Center will find much to interest them and exposure makes them feel the importance of art to many people, both those who create and those who appreciate.

Participation in Art Events

There are many art festivals, art parades, fence paintings in which the Center should participate. They are not always the most significant art forms of our time, but they are enjoyable and stimulating. These events can be of untold value when a student determines he wishes his art to be represented and participates wholeheartedly.

Many cities, art organizations, radio and television stations have yearly arts and crafts festivals. These are excellent places for students to display and sell their work. Students can man the tables and exhibits, thus meeting the public and becoming a part of the art community.

11 The Art Gallery and Exhibition

As soon as possible, the Center should establish an art gallery. Ideally, the gallery should be in a separate area in the Center or in a totally separate space adjacent to or near the Center. Probably the best solution is having a divided building with separate entrances—a space for the studio and a space for the gallery. This allows free flow between the two and yet does not cause disruption in the studio by constant coming and going by those particularly interested in the gallery. Until such time as this ideal arrangement can be established, it may be necessary to maintain a "gallery" using the walls of the studio for changing exhibitions.

Once a gallery is established, it should be maintained in a professional manner with a curator in charge, having time-limited exhibitions, announcements of the shows, and public openings.

The most important function of the gallery is to exhibit the work of the Center's students. The beauty, the expressiveness, the vision and the genuine artistic creations of their work must be seen in a professional setting to be really understood. At times the shows may be of one artist's work, at other times of a group of artists. It is very different seeing the works in process in the studio and seeing them hung professionally in the gallery. For both the student artists and the visitors the art takes on a special significance in the gallery setting.

For the student there is tremendous pride in seeing one's work valued and deserving of an exhibit. It gives the student a chance to see a group of his paintings professionally displayed and an opportunity to see his own growth as an artist. It also gives him an opportunity to discuss his work if he is able to do so, with visitors and artists who come to the gallery. It transforms him from a second-class citizen to a person regarded highly in the community.

For a visitor it shatters the stereotype of handicapped people. Both the public and professionals cannot fail to appreciate the quality and expressiveness of the art.

The gallery of course also provides a place where the art work can attract a buyer or someone who may want to rent the work for his home or office.

Gallery Exhibits

Artist Students:
- Sequential paintings, prints and sculpture of an individual student or group of students showing their development
- Individual art exhibits
- Group art exhibits
- Comparison of art work of disabled students with work of illustrious artists
- Variety of art styles in the work of different artist-students
- Exhibits based on one theme

Photographic Essays:
- Building the Center: how the building looked, how it was remodeled, how it now looks in operation
- Students at work: intensity and concentration; joy of working and of accomplishment

o   Activities of students during one day
o   Special events

Outside Artists

Many outstanding artists are not only willing but proud to have a joint show with gifted artists of the Center. These artists must believe in the artistic quality of the work of the artist-student for them to show their work in the same space. Each artist stands on his own merit. Both are shown on an equal footing. This is a new concept and must be maintained for public acceptance of artists with disabilities.

Outside Shows in the Gallery

Very often museums, galleries, art associations, private collectors, and other Art Centers will send shows to the gallery. Students are able to visit again and again and study the art at their leisure.

If the gallery is secure, has an attendant at all times, has locked cases, and has insurance, it will be much easier to convince such institutions to lend their work to the Art Center. Exhibits such as masks, costumes, paintings, sculpture, prints, jewelry, glass, pottery, etc., would be of great educational value and interest to the students and to others.

Exhibits Outside the Center

Since most Art Centers will have to be in operation for some time before they can afford a professional gallery, it becomes essential to establish a constant flow of outside exhibits to maintain the image of the Art Center in the community, to establish the students' pride in their work, and to sell their work.

All possible sites for exhibits should be carefully selected so that the dignity of the art is not sacrificed. All shows should be publicized in a professional manner, using press releases, public service announcements, and, whenever possible, invitations. Press should be invited as well as television, theater, cinema, and radio personalities.

Excellent places to show art are in art galleries, lobbies of corporations, social agencies, other Art Centers, universities and colleges, theater lobbies, other public
buildings, and dignified shopping malls. Places that should be avoided are supermarkets, private business offices, inaccessible areas, and places without adequate protection from vandalism and the weather.

Students' work should be entered in both juried and nonjuried shows together with all artists.

After the Center is well established, it is important not only to have local shows. Exhibits of national importance should be planned, implemented and shown throughout the United States.

The Curator

A Curator should be appointed to select and prepare art exhibits with the help of the staff. Art shows in the gallery, in the community, in libraries, public buildings, shopping centers, store windows, museums and galleries must be implemented. A curator should also prepare traveling shows.

First-rate art from a handicapped artist

By Charles Shere
Tribune Art Critic

The two-person show currently at Oakland's Creative Growth gallery (355 24th St.) raises some important questions about art — questions this center has raised before, but rarely so pointedly.

Creative Growth is a center offering art studio facilities to handicapped persons — in many oases, persons who have until this experience been in no position to realize they are artists.

Their handicaps range from severe physical limitations to severe mental ones. They are, of course, of varying skill and genius, as are all artists. But among them are some real naturals, artists with distinctive gifts of vision, composition and expression.

The gallery has long wanted to exhibit these artists alongside recognized artists, and the current show is such an installation:

GALLERY ROUNDUP

paintings by Betty Kano, a well-known abstractionist who is not handicapped, and by Arlene Tuur, a Creative Growth artist.

Kano's work looks plain and minimal on first glance, but opens into rich, subtly poetic vistas as you investigate it further. The most impressive pieces are three triptychs — square canvases mounted adjacent in a horizontal row — all called "Integrations." The one subtitled "Red, White and Blue" is the simplest: a black square on the left, streaked subtly with red; a blue-black one on the right; at center, a rose-pink square.

"Integration/Synthesis" reveals most clearly Kano's technique, which is the nuanced use of color after-images. An ochre left-hand square anchors a vibrant orange one barred with bright green; between them a

blue-purple square contains a calligraphic gesture with slight implications of the human figure.

Kano's painting is absorbing and deep. But across the floor it is Arlene Tuur's work which is really exciting — particularly at a time when "New Expressionism" is the latest gallery trend.

Tuur's work is real expressionism. She works in tempera, or felt-pen, or watercolor, envisioning a lyrical world teeming with tiny cell-like shapes. Her palette runs to oranges, reds, pinks and violets, and the surfaces are broken up into what looks like an allover, almost obsessive outline-and-fill-in pattern.

These details resolve, though, into magical landscapes, occasionally with ghosts of figures or faces emerging from them. The

compositions are unique and wonderfully controlled, balanced between energetic vibration and calm, ordered balance. There are no weak passages, and there is a masterly sense of distant and middle distance.

The question is, can Tuur be an artist although she must work outside the world of galleries and museums? Can her paintings, priced in the middle two-digit range, compete in any way with Kano's, which run 15 times as expensive? How do the market, society, culture and the prison of personal handicap interact?

BETTY KANO
PAINTINGS

JANUARY 6-FEBRUARY 18

ARLENE TUUR
PAINTINGS
PRINTS

RECEPTION THURSDAY,
JANUARY 13, 5-7 P.M.

GALLERY HOURS MONDAY-FRIDAY, 10-4

CREATIVE GROWTH GALLERY   355 24TH STREET, OAKLAND

THE TRIBUNE
Tuesday, February 8, 1983

If this work is left to the teachers or the Director, it may become of secondary importance. Exhbiting work is the primary function of the curator. It is a full time job to schedule art exhibits, keep records of the artists' work, keep up the slide collection, and sell the work of the artists.

The curator must establish and maintain all the professional aspects of the art gallery, including announcements and exciting, different shows to attract untapped audiences. So many interesting shows, unusual openings, methods of display, and ways of interacting with the community can be devised by an imaginative curator.

Permanent Collection

The Center should maintain and make available a permanent collection of the best work of artist-students and other interesting work showing their growth. Best presevation techniques should be used.

It is of prime importance to the Center to have available slides and photographs. Slides of the artist-students' work are often called for to enter exhibits, to obtain grants, and for lectures, workshops and teaching. It is necessary to have available the progress of each student for review purposes and to show to interested people.

Slides should be made of exhibits, special events, the development of the Center. Slides should be used as a source of art education for the Center's artist-students. A collection should be maintained of historical, contemporary, ethnic, folk and outsider art.

Photographs are important for all the above as well as for publications and exhibits.

III.
Making The Creative Art Center Happen

Chapters 12-21

Beverly Pruett

12 Starting an Art Center for People with Disabilities

The key to immediate and long-term support of an Art Center for disabled people lies in active involvement of the community. The community as we describe it consists of disabled and nondisabled people who live or work in the neighborhood or geographical area or who have a special interest in the Art Center. The Community also includes agencies, schools, organizations, and businesses.

To establish an Art Center, members of the community must recognize the need for an Art Center for people with disabilities and must be committed to assist in establishing the Art Center. They must be ready to help break down negative stereotypes of disabled people, influence others to accept disabled people in their neighborhood, and must remove physical and psychological barriers preventing disabled people from participarting in community activities.

Starting an Art Center

Art Centers may begin in various ways. Following are two examples:

In one community a bus driver for a school for handicapped children noticed an older man who seemed to be mentally retarded sitting on the steps of a nearby building. She approached him and asked what he did. He said, "I sit here." Upon further inquiry she found that this was true—Joseph had nothing to do.

She talked to him a number of times and found that what he really liked to do was paint. He showed her a sketch he had made. She made inquiries and learned there was no program for him. She reported this man's need to her sister, a psychiatric social worker. Her sister brought this information to her supervisor, who had visited Art Centers for disabled people in other cities. The supervisor made an informal survey and discovered many older disabled people were very interested in art but no program existed.

She called a meeting of artists and special education teachers to discuss establishing an Art Center for disabled people. Committees were formed to get the project off the ground. Local newspapers picked up the theme and reproduced Joseph's work with stories about the need for an Art Center. Many people joined and the establishment of an Art Center for disabled people was well on its way.

* * * *

Mary Jo taught art twice a week in a large state hospital near her home. The excellent results were amazing to everyone. The local art association showed her students' work in their art gallery. When her students were discharged from the state hospital, they were placed in sheltered workshops where art programs did not exist. Mary Jo was concerned that her artist/students no longer had any opportunity for art work. She spoke to her friends in the art association, including some who were very influential in the community. They too were very concerned and suggested she set up an Art Center where her students could continue their work.

Mary Jo was excited about the prospect and enlisted the help of friends. After assessing the practicality of such an Art Center, the group formed a Board of Directors.

Involving the Community

Members of the community serve as a broad support system. They can be called upon to act as volunteers, raise funds, publicize the Art Center, and/or serve as advocates. They can scrounge the neighborhood for needed supplies and materials, sponsor fund-raising events, help find appropriate space, and move the Art Center into that space.

Members of the community can play a number of roles at the Art Center. They can serve on the Board of Directors, provide financial and political support, and refer appropriate students to the Art Center.

Ideally, even before the Art Center is established, the entire community should be actively involved. However, this is rarely the case. Usually a few interested people and organizations, enlightened parents, and/or disabled people see the need for setting up an Art Center and start groping for help. Regularly scheduled meetings are essential to bring interested persons together to discuss the problems and make decisions.

Members of this interested nucleus must begin to involve others, since the setting up of an Art Center is a complex and time-consuming process, and is dependent on a strong, wide base. The more extensively the community is involved, the more likely a successful Art Center will be established and the more likely it is to survive. One of the major tasks during this phase is to identify "movers and shakers" capable and willing to carry out responsible tasks. As soon as possible public meetings in accessible schools, libraries, centers should be held to discuss needs, implementation, and to recruit more people. At these meetings it is important to determine the philosophy and structure of the Art Center: Who it will serve and where it should be located.

Some well-intentioned groups have foundered at this early stage owing to the inability of persons in the nuclear group to work together in dealing with these problems. In order to make progress, these problems must be resolved.

Once there is basic agreement as to philosophy and structure, the nuclear group must determine the best location for the Art Center, sources of funding, how best to publicize the Art Center, what staff is needed. Since each of these problems is complex, it may be essential to form committees to work on different aspects and report back to the nuclear group.

Funds must be obtained for immediate needs, such as printing, postage, stationery, transportation, phone calls, etc. It has been our experience in working with groups at this stage that there is a wide variation in expertise in raising this money. Some groups raise small amounts of cash through flea markets, cake sales, dinner parties at people's homes, and personal solicitations from church groups, service clubs, parents and relatives of disabled people. Others have held special events such as movies, plays, and picnics. Still others have asked friends, neighbors, and family for contributions.

In this early stage in the development of the Art Center it is essential to involve the entire community.

Choosing a Board of Directors

As community support and interest for an Art Center begin to coalesce, a more permanent structure is needed. This is the time to form a Board of Directors.

The Board of Directors is the policy making and governing body of the Art Center. It is responsible for a dynamic, creative, and quality organization. The Board should both initiate

James Boutell

San Francisco Examiner August 17, 1986

Image

The Magazine of Northern California

Art With a Difference: Wondrous Works From Disabled Artists

The walls explode in a riot of color. Marvelous shapes, bold, breathless, jagged lines come at you in a rush. A smell of paint hovers in the air. There are assemblages, montages, pieces of sculpture. In a corner hangs a painting of a swan —a bird so serene, so lovely, you can almost imagine it floating in a dream.

In many ways it's a typical artist's workshop, but with one important difference. This art is done by people with severe developmental problems—men and women who are mentally disabled, emotionally disabled, physically disabled, and sometimes all three.

And yet out of this comes a wondrous beauty—a beauty that you can behold this month in San Francisco at the Chevron Gallery and the Marina Bank of America.

"People actually buy these pictures without knowing that the artists are retarded. They don't buy out of charity, but because the art appeals to them so much," say Florence Ludins-Katz, co-founder of the Institute of Art and Disabilities in Richmond, where all this creativity takes place.

Mrs. Katz, a painter, and her husband, Elias, a retired clinical psychologist, started the center two years ago, although the inspiration for it goes back to 1974. Appalled by what they saw retarded people doing in so-called "sheltered" workshops, she and Dr. Katz decided there must be something wrong. "These people were performing mindless, repetitive work," she recalls, "things that were too low for normal workers, or things that could be done cheaper by humans than by machines. Folding papers, pulling out staples. Pure rote."

The Katzes began taking disabled people into their Berkeley home, teaching them the rudiments of art. Eventually, the small groups grew to include more than 120 budding artists, prompting the Katzes to start a center in Oakland, which they called Creative Growth. In 1982, having showed that the concept works, the Katzes moved on— "because," she says, "we needed to replicate the program in other places."

Since then, they have opened art centers for the disabled in San Francisco (Creativity Explored), San Jose (Creativity Unlimited) and now Richmond.

Everywhere they've gone, miracles have happened. "We've found in these people— some so severely retarded they have no speech, no communication whatsoever— that when you give them encouragement and time and and love and materials to function with, they do so. Every day is a surprise to us. Every day brings breakthroughs. It might take a day, it might take a year before we see anything, but it does take place."

Mrs. Katz cites a young woman named Anita who started by simply dabbing one color on top of another. "You would say mindless, repetitive, but there was a glimmer of joy in what she was doing. There was a very definite relationship between her and the art. Suddenly, after about four months, instead of just undifferentiated masses, shapes began emerging. Then color could be seen within the shapes, and a painting developed, as beautiful as anything by a professional."

Indeed, on several occasions student works have been accepted by juried art shows. Last year, for example, among the 95 works selected for the Richmond Art Center's exhibition, twelve were by disabled artists. "Our people were able to compete on a professional, artistic level," says Mrs. Katz proudly. "Of course, we take the same care as we would with a professional's picture and we watch the students very closely as they develop from one stage to another."

But how explain the success of this art, by people who had previously known only failure?

Evidently, it's the nature of the artists themselves. "Everything is very direct," says sculptor Larry Stefle, one of three professional artists who teach at the center. "And that's what impresses you—the spontaneity of it, the uninhibited quality. These people are not worried about getting into galleries. They just do what they want to do."

The 2,700-square-foot center in Richmond is now a home away from home for some twenty artists, all of whom live on Supplemental Security Income and are brought there in mini-buses. The Katzes earn no salary. It costs about $120,000 a year to operate the center, and they generally come up around $2,000 short, the deficit being made up with grants, rummage sales and the occasional gift.

Already, the center is too small. The Katzes have ordered a press for lithographs and etchings and are wondering where to put it. They would like to have a gallery, too. This year alone, there have been 23 shows of student works, in places ranging from Alta Bates Hospital in Berkeley to San Francisco's Nanny Goat Hill Gallery.

One of the center's most significant achievements is redefining some long-cherished notions about the relationship between talent and IQ. "The young woman who painted that swan can't even write," says Florence Katz. "Just her name. What that tells me is that the IQ level assigned people is false. IQ tests a certain type of intelligence, but not the whole person. In our society we tend to take a person and cut him up in pieces. I say: Let's look at the whole person. The development of a person through art is the most remarkable thing."

The next showing of art from the Institute of Arts and Disabilities opens on August 20 and runs through September 5 at the Chevron Gallery, 555 Market Street, San Francisco. The gallery is open 9 a.m. to 5 p.m., Monday through Saturday. Institute works are also on display through August 22 at the Marina branch of the Bank of America, 2460 Lombard Street, San Francisco. Visitors are also welcome at the institute, 233 South 41st Street, Richmond, but are asked to call 620-0290 in advance.

WALTER BLUM

The striking works by disabled artists at the Richmond Institute of Arts and Disabilities include (above) a fanciful scene by Angela Campbell and (left) a vivid abstract by Sylvia Fragoso.

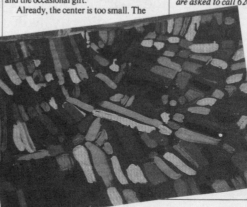

August 17, 1986/IMAGE

IMAGE magazine article

and be responsive to new ideas. Its ongoing job is to insure immediate and long-term survival of the organization. This is accomplished by digging its roots deeply into the community and responding to community needs.

The selection of the Board is of utmost importance. At this stage, the Board's highest priority is to activate the Art Center. When considering individuals for Board membership, expertise and characteristics must be scrutinized with one question in mind: "In what ways will this person help make the Art Center a reality?"

The most important qualification of good Board members is dedication to the establishment of the Art Center. They must recognize the importance of quality programming for disabled persons. Board members must be willing to make their time, talents, contacts and specific skills available for the organization. They must be aware of the program's goals and operation through direct observation, discussion, and written materials. They must attend Board meetings (usually once a month, more often at the beginning), should participate as members of committees, and should support programs, affairs, and activities of the Art Center. They should see themselves as advocates for this program in their business, professional, political and social activities. They must be dedicated to maintain and improve the quality and financing of the program.

Important questions to ask potential Board members include:

o   Does he understand the real need for such an Art Center?
o   Can he and will he help raise funds through professional, business, political, and friendship contacts?
o   Does his name add prestige and credibility to the organization—politically, socially, intellectually, economically?
o   Is he a representative of the disabled community?
o   Does he represent or have contacts with minority groups?
o   Does he have the needed practical and professional expertise in dealing with the community?
o   Does he have expertise in establishing new enterprises?
o   Once the enterprise is established, will he help maintain high quality control for the organization?

Once established, the Board of Directors assumes responsibility for the Art Center. The Board must continue to work directly with the original group of interested persons and organizations.

The Board must not become frustrated if movement is slow or community action less than encouraging. In these initial organizational stages, this should be expected: There is no program to show and a lot must be taken on faith.

As the Board clarifies the underlying ideas of the Art Center, publicizes the Art Center, actively investigates possible sites, raises seed money to start the program, writes grants for the establishment of a permanent program, plans for special events, and maintains lines of communication with the community, its members will develop a group process. Each successful step lends credibility to the enterprise.

Letterhead stationery should be prepared with the name of the organization, address, phone number, Board members and affiliations and those of the advisory group. Nonprofit, tax-exempt status should be noted. This stationery establishes permanence and credibility for the organization.

TASKS OF THE
BOARD OF DIRECTORS

Setting up a Nonprofit Tax-exempt Corporation

While other forms of organization are possible, establishing the Art Center as a nonprofit tax-exempt corporation is the most practical and widely used approach. These corporations are established under state and federal statutes for public benefit and not for private gain. This status makes it possible for the organization to be exempt from taxation, and qualify for government grants and grants from foundations. It also enables the organization to receive contributions of money, property, and other valuable assets from private donors (corporations, associations, individuals) who receive a tax deduction for their gifts. This tax deduction encourages contributions.

Nonprofit tax-exempt corporations vary but they all have certain things in common. All must be incorporated within a state. Bylaws must be prepared which spell out the goals of the corporation and the duties and responsibilities of the Board of Directors, the officers, and the members.

Incorporation is a legal process which provides credibility. It should be completed as early as possible, since it sets up a legal entity responsible for the Art Center and makes possible the receiving and expending of funds. Funds are subject to audit, and adequate financial records must be maintained. Since incorporation is a legal process, a lawyer should be engaged for the process.

Formulating Goals of the Art Center

The Board of Directors must formulate goals for the Art Center as early as possible, since the goals are part of the Articles of Incorporation. To obtain community support, the goals should be publicized. Chapter 4 includes a comprehensive list of goals. Each Art Center can choose or adapt those goals which seem best suited to its needs.

Defining the Population to be Served

Persons with disabilities can be defined in legal, medical, or functional terms. The definitions do not always coincide. For our purposes, those with disabilities are defined as those children and adults who cannot function normally in the usual environment because of physical, intellectual, emotional, and/or social handicaps. Any community has large numbers of such persons with disabilities.

Most children with disabilities attend school and cannot attend an Art Center during the day. From a practical point of view the full-time program of the Art Center is limited to adults with disabilities. This does not preclude a part-time, after-school, weekend, or summer program for children and/or adolescents.

In order for the Art Center function, the Board must define the population the Art Center is to serve. This should include the disabilities served, the age of the participants, and any exclusionary factors (destructive to themselves or others, incontinent, unable to profit from the program, or any other standards the Board may set).

Clarifying Space Needs, Locating a Site, and Acquiring the Building

The site of the Art Center is a factor in the success of the Center. In locating a site, the Board must consider both the neighborhood and the building itself.

The Art Center should be in a nonthreatening neighborhood that is not isolated. It should be easily accessible by public transportation. The students should be able to walk freely about the neighborhood without fear of being abused physically or psychologically. A nearby park or museum would be delightful.

In most situations it is wiser to rent than to purchase during the start-up period. This is a trial period and much must be learned about space needed, number of students to be served, financial and community support, and appropriateness of the neighborhood for the program. Purchasing a building means a long-term commitment to a particular location.

These considerations must be weighed against the advantages of purchase: renovations need be made only once, a feeling of permanence develops about the organization, and the financial investment in the building may increase rapidly. Funds for renovation of a purchased building may be easier to obtain from individuals, foundations, and government agencies than for renovation of a rented space.

Appropriate buildings which usually require minimum renovation include former commercial store fronts, supermarkets, automobile show rooms, furniture stores, railroad stations. The space must be fully accessible for wheelchairs, and able to pass all regulations and codes—such as zoning, fire, health, building. Remodeling may be necessary to meet these requirements.

Inappropriate spaces include small private homes, office space above the ground floor, former hospitals with small rooms, dilapidated buildings with intricate exits and entrances, church basements, and polluted or noisy areas. It is also inappropriate to share space with other organizations which will have priority claims, even though the space may be otherwise suitable. The Art Center must not be viewed as a second-class citizen.

The possibility of obtaining space at no cost or at low cost should be explored. Occasionally government agencies and schools have surplus buildings or space available at little or no cost. The assistance of realtors and interested Board members should be actively sought. However, under no circumstances should the Art Center's needs be compromised solely to save money. The isolation, poverty, physical danger, and/or inadequacy of certain locations make it impossible to run a high-quality Art Center. Before a decision is made, all these matters must be thoroughly investigated by the Board.

Licensing the Art Center

In most states the Art Center must have a license to operate. Licensing requirements differ from state to state, and counties and cities often have further regulations. Before committing to a space, check that the site meets all local, state, and federal licensing regulations on zoning, safety, building construction, toilet facilities, number of people permitted in the building, fire, health, etc. It is desirable to obtain prior informal approval from the appropriate agencies to avoid costly and time-consuming delays in obtaining a license.

Raising "Seed Money" and Laying the Groundwork for Future Financial Support

Ideally, "seed money" to set up the Art Center should be readily available either from public or private sources. Unfortunately, this is rarely the case. Seeking and obtaining start-up funds becomes a critical task. Many wonderful ideas have been abandoned due to lack of funding at this stage. Despite the difficulties, if the idea has merit—with persistence, organization, research as to funding sources, and widespread community support, funding will ultimately be found.

Just what does "seed money" mean? It is the actual cash needed to set up and keep a program going for a period of about three months, or until the start of regular funding. After the start-up period, the program must obtain regular ongoing income, e.g., contracts, fees for service, grants, contributions.

A typical list of start-up expenses includes one-time and continuing costs:

One-Time Costs

o   Incorporation fees
o   Licensing fees (vary from state to state)
o   Renovation
o   Furniture
o   Office equipment: typewriter, desks, chairs, filing cabinets, bookcases, xerox machine, calculator, computer, etc.
o   Art equipment: tables, chairs, easels, cabinets, tools, printing press, framing and matting equipment, paper cutter, kiln, camera, video equipment
o   Kitchen equipment: stove, refrigerator, cabinets, tables
o   Installation of utilities and equipment

Continuing Costs

o   Salaries: Director, art teacher(s), curator, secretary, attendant and other staff
o   Rent or mortgage payment
o   Utilities: telephone, gas, electricity, water
o   Travel by staff: speaking engagements, recruiting students, conferences and meetings
o   Office supplies: stationery, bookkeeping supplies
o   Art supplies: paper, paints, clay, brushes, felt pens, crayons
o   Framing and matting supplies
o   Postage and art freight charges
o   Printing of stationery, brochures, newsletters, gallery announcements
o   Housekeeping supplies

The amount of "seed money" needed will vary greatly according to the location, the condition of the building, the number of persons to be served, salary levels for the staff in the area, and the scrounging ability of those interested in the Art Center.

A reasonable figure at this writing (1989) for a start-up period of three months for a group of 15 students is about $25,000 (see Table 12-1, Sample Budget During Start-Up Period). This figure can be considerably reduced if free furniture, space, remodeling, equipment, supplies, and volunteer help can be obtained. In some communities it is possible to obtain assistance from local construction unions or military units (Naval Construction Battalions, National Guard, Civilian Conservation Corps), or service clubs. Surplus property may be available from public schools, universities, the Army, city, county, state and federal agencies, and from individuals and corporations.

How Can "Seed Money" Be Obtained?

The fastest source of "seed money" is a wealthy benefactor or a group of benefactors who are extremely interested in establishing an Art Center for people with disabilities. This sometimes happens but is rare.

There is no sure way to obtain "seed money." Individuals must choose those methods which are most suited to them. Often local foundations or foundations that cater primarily to the local area or the state may be contacted. These foundations are often interested in start-up grants for space renovation and initial program development. Local foundations may ultimately become involved in continuing support as they may be willing to make annual grants to the support of the general program. They can be located through the Directory of Foundations in most public libraries.

It may be possible to enlist the local community welfare agency, especially if you develop a joint plan with some of the organizations dedicated to helping persons with disabilities, e.g., United Cerebral Palsy, Associations for Retarded Citizens, local self-help centers, and so forth. Persons from these organizations should be included on your board.

It is easy to become discouraged during this start-up period and feel that funds will never be obtained. Our experience has been that many well-intentioned people give up and drop out, only to try again when they feel the Art Center has a chance of becoming a reality. This is the time when the Board must make a special effort to maintain morale by publicizing the program and involving as many people as possible.

It is often helpful to contact an existing Art Center—existing Centers can provide written material, exhibits, and slide shows. Prospective donors can visit these programs to gain a better understanding of what their own community Art Center can offer.

Laying the Groundwork for Future Financial Support

The work done and the experience gained in obtaining "seed money" should be seen as part of a continuing fund-raising process, since there will never be a time when funds will not be needed for carrying on and developing the work of the Art Center.

Many organizations and individuals who were not ready to support a program still in its conceptual stage may be willing to help an existing, on-going Art Center. Also, persons and organizations who gave during the start-up stages may feel encouraged by seeing the Center's accomplishments, and should be contacted as sources of continuing support.

A program of "Charter Supporters" can be established as well as contributors to a Building Fund for space development.

A Budget for a Three-Month Period

One of the first tasks of the Board is to prepare a "start-up" budget detailing anticipated income and expenditures (see Table 12-1, Sample Budget During Start-Up Period). This budget is extremely important for planning, soliciting necessary funds to get the Art Center off the ground, and establishing the credibility of the organization. Budget expenditures should be realistic—neither exaggerating costs, which makes the project appear impractical, nor underestimating expenses to make the Art Center appear more affordable. The anticipated income should also be realistic, with knowledge of the sources and amounts which can be obtained both immediately and in the long run.

During the first three months of operation, absolute minimum costs usually include salaries (the Director, art teacher, secretary, and attendant) and operating costs (rent, telephone, utilities, art and office equipment and supplies, travel, printing and postage). While donations may fill some of these needs, it is essential to prepare a budget which does not depend on this possibility.

A Proposed Budget for the First Full Year of Operation

Once the expenses and income for a three-month start-up period have been compared with actual operating costs, it is easy to develop a budget for a full year of normal operation (see Table 12-2, Proposed Annual Budget for 30 Students). Income is more difficult to estimate. Searching for and obtaining funds is a constant necessity.

The Director is responsible for preparing the budget and then submitting it to the Board of Directors for approval.

Publicizing the New Art Center

Support for an Art Center for people with disabilities will come from an enlightned public. People must fully understand the necessity for establishing the Art Center and the need for continuing support. Therefore a plan to educate the pulbic must be developed and maintained. Public meetings, special events, workshops, articles in newspapers and magazines, radio shows and television appearances must be arranged. Until art work is available from the new Art Center, exhibits of the work of students from other Art Centers or of artists with disabilities in the community can be held in banks, libraries, museums, art galleries, and public and corporate buildings. In some communities, large corporations may be willing to allow their public relations staff to contribute time to publicizing the Art Center.

The Board Adopts a Personnel Manual

The Board of Directors establishes the Personnel Manual, which includes job descriptions and agency regulations (see Appendix C). It includes rights benefits and grievance procedures.

The Board Selects and Appoints the Director

The key staff member and the one who must be identified as soon as possible is the Director. A Director sets the tone of the whole organization.

Choosing a Director of the Art Center

A major responsibility of the Board is to appoint and evaluate the Director, who is directly responsible for carrying out the philosophy and policies of the Board.

TABLE 12-1

Sample Budget During Start-Up Period (1989)

		1st Month	2nd Month	3rd Month
Number of Students in Program		0	10	15
Expenditures				
Salaries	*Salary Range/Year*			
Director	15,000 - 18,000	1,500	1,500	1,500
Art Teacher	12,000 - 15,000	—	1,200	1,200
Attendant/Aide	7,000 - 9,000	—	800	800
Secretary	9,000 - 11,000	900	900	900
Maintenance	1,200	100	100	100
		2,500	4,500	4,500
Fringe Benefits (15%)		360	660	660
Total Salaries/Fringe Benefits		2,860	5,160	5,160
Operating Costs* Annual Costs				
Incorporation (legal fees)		500	—	—
Rent	$12,000	1,000	1,000	1,000
Utilities (heat, light, phone)	6,000	500	500	500
Mileage (staff)	1,200	100	100	100
Equipment (art: tables, racks)	2,000	500	500	100
Equipment (office: desks, type-writer, etc.)	2,000	500	500	100
Art Supplies: (paints, paper, clay, etc.)	2,000	500	500	100
Office Supplies	1,000	100	100	100
Miscellaneous: (printing,duplicating, postage, etc.)	2,000	150	150	150
Total Operating Costs		3,850	3,350	2,150
Total Salaries and Operating Costs		6,710	9,510	7,310
Total Expenditrues for 3-Month Startup Period				$23,530

* No funds provided for remodeling.

TABLE 12-2

Proposed Annual Budget for 30 Students (1989)

EXPENDITURES (Estimated)

Personnel Costs

Director	18,000
Art Instructor	14,400
Art Instructor	14,400
Social Worker	14,400
Attendant/Aide	9,000
Secretary	10,000
Maintenance	1,200
Accounting	1,000
Total	82,400
Fringe	12,360

Total Personnel Costs   94,760

Operating Costs

Rent ($1,000/month)	12,000
Utilities (heat, light, phone)	6,000
Transportation (staff)	1,000
Art Equipment	2,000
Office Equipment	2,000
Art Supplies	2,000
Office Supplies	1,000
Miscellaneous	2,000

Total Operating Costs   28,000

TOTAL PERSONNEL AND OPERATING COSTS   122,760

INCOME (Estimated)

Fees and contracts for services provided to students	75,000
Constributions	
Corporations	15,000
Foundations	15,000
Individuals	5,000
Memberships	8,000
Other	5,000

TOTAL INCOME   122,760

13 Obtaining Continuing Financial Support

Assuming that "seed money" is available for the first few months, one of the first responsibilities of the Director, with the strong assistance of the Board, is to insure ongoing financial support for the Art Center. No program, however essential, can exist without a consistent financial base.

An Art Center should not be dependent on one source of funding. A funding source can dry up or may be considerably reduced. There is seldom enough money given to a program by one source to provide all the necessary costs. Very often funding sources change their priorities, and even if the Center is doing an excellent job this source may not continue to support the Center. A variety of sources make the Art Center better able to survive.

A successful Art Center must define and pursue many diverse sources of funds. In fundraising, imagination and innovation may work where the usual methods fail. The Board of Directors and the Director need to identify government sources and private donors. Persons with appropriate skills, knowledge, and contacts must be involved in approaching corporations, foundations, business associates, and personal friends.

To increase giving from these sources, the Director should keep funders and potential funders informed of the Art Center's activities. Supporters should be invited to visit the Art Center, observe progress and the programs, and be kept abreast of what is being planned. A newsletter and articles in the press are excellent means of sharing such information.

As the organization grows, the Art Center may want to hire a part- or full-time fund raiser or public relations person to coordinate fund raising and publicity efforts.

Fees for Services

One source of funding for the Art Center is to establish a fee for the services provided. The fee for services can be determined by dividing the total cost of the program by the number of participants.

In our experience working with low-income students in urban areas, no more than one out of fifty students has personal resources to pay fees. However, affluent communities may present a different picture.

Since most disabled people are on Supplementary Security Income (SSI) and cannot afford to pay the necessary fees, it is essential to find one or more government agencies which will pay the fees, either through a contract or a fee-for-service arrangement.

Most government agencies compute fees for service by means of a formula and it is almost impossible to make changes once the fee is set. From a practical viewpoint, it is wise to set the initial fee for service as realistically as possible.

It should be emphasized that fees for service will never cover the Art Center's total expenses. There are people with disabilities the Art Center serves who do not qualify under government regulations. In any program unexpected expenses arise during the year. A substantial part of the total costs of running the regular program must be obtained through fund raising efforts.

GRANTS

An important supplementary source of funds is in the form of grants from government agencies, foundations, and corporations. Often these require matching contributions from the applicant organization. Certainly a program cannot be run on grants alone.

Grants from Governmental Agencies

Most grants from federal, state, county, city or local governments are limited to one to three years. If the grant is made for more than one year it is usually necessary to reapply annually.

These grants are highly competitive. Often the applicant organization is required to be in existence for one or more years prior to the application date. Even for those who are successful there may be a considerable time lapse from the date of application to the receipt of funds.

Grants from Foundations and Corporations

Many large and small foundations and corporations have regular cycles for reviewing and making grants. In some instances the cycle may be a few weeks, but mostly the funding cycle is six months to a year. These are extremely competitive.

As with government grants, funds are usually provided for a specific period or for a special purpose (equipment, capital outlay, etc.). In some grants there is a provision for grant continuation for an additional period of time.

Generally speaking, grants from corporations and foundations are more flexible than government grants in terms of requirements, funding cycles, and amounts granted. Often the funds are managed by executives who have wide latitude in making these decisions. Corporations which make large grants may also make small grants to organizations in communities where their subsidiaries or branches operate.

There are numerous publications, libraries, and grantsmanship organizations which provide assistance in applying for grants at low cost or no cost. Directories can be located, with the help of librarians, that will identify prospective corporate and foundation donors.

Memberships

Dues-paying members represent important community support for the Center. Even though there are many persons who can afford to make only a small payment for membership fees, the number of members gives some indication of public interest and involvement in the program. This is especially important to show community support when applying for grants and contributions.

Income from membership fees cannot be sufficient to support the Center. Indeed, the costs of obtaining new members and retaining old members may be so high there is very little left for supporting the program. Nevertheless, it is essential to maintain the membership as a means of broadening the constituencies which will support the organization in ways beyond the actual financial help provided by the membership fee. For example, members frequently inform their friends about the Center, thereby involving more people in eventual support of the program. Also, members may run benefits, may attend open houses, and may conduct social functions for the organization. Members have a stake in the organization. All memberships should be acknowledged.

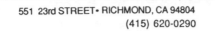

NATIONAL INSTITUTE OF **ART & DISABILITIES**

551 23rd STREET • RICHMOND, CA 94804
(415) 620-0290

NEWSLETTER - SUMMER 1985

The Institute of Art and Disabilities is now
functioning smoothly. Under the direction
and inspiration of the excellent teaching
staff, our students are showing remarkable
progress in their art, in their socialization,
and in their personal growth.

We have already outgrown our space although we
do not yet have the number of students that
would enable us to operate at maximum efficien-
cy. We estimate that we will achieve this number by the end of the year. Although our
building is pleasant, light, and airy, it is
inadequate. We have no storage space, no office
space, no space for our clay work or kiln and no
space for an art press. Above all, we are unable
to start our graduate training program or establish an art gallery, both keystones in the total
concept of the Institute.

One of our greatest priorities is moving to a
building that will meet our needs. We have
decided to purchase, if possible, rather than
to rent. The El Cerrito Plaza benefit sale
raised over $3,000.00 which has been designated
as the beginning of our building fund. We must
raise at least $50,000.00 for a down payment on
a building. We cannot do this without your help.
We welcome your ideas, your participation, and
your financial help to make this dream a reality.

Lisa Camacho
Student of Institute of Art and Disabilities

Fund Raising Events

There are many regular and special events which can raise funds for the organization. Certain events take place annually, while others occur according to the inclination and interest of individuals or groups. For example, an annual art auction of work contributed by professional artists and craftsmen in the community or contributed by the students of the Center may provide a substantial amount. Other artistic fund raising benefit events are concerts and theater performances.

Then there are informal and fun events such as "A Day at the Races," cake sales, flea markets, and garage sales. For example, the Oakland Museum raises part of its costs through a gigantic week-long "White Elephant Sale" which uses a large volunteer force working all year and involving the whole community.

Sales of Art Work Produced by Artist-Students

Paintings, sculpture, and other art work produced by participants can be sold. Although it is a good idea for the artist-students to receive most of the money, a small fraction can be retained by the Center to pay for frames and preparation of art work for sale. Certain special events, such as a Christmas sale of participants' work, can be designated for fund raising purposes. It is unlikely that revenue from this source will provide more than a small fraction of the Center's expenses. Nevertheless, there are great benefits to the participants' self-esteem and feelings of worth in realizing that they are helping support the Center and that others value their art enough to purchase it.

Direct Solicitation

Individuals, service organizations, businesses, and church groups may make gifts of money, stocks or bonds, equipment, and supplies. Since the Center is a nonprofit, tax-exempt corporation, all contributions offer income tax advantages to the donor.

Wills, Bequests, Trusts, Annuities

Every effort should be made to solicit funds in wills, bequests, trusts, and annuities. Many organizations make a concerted effort to obtain these gifts as excellent long-term support. This type of support gives a feeling of permanency to the organization.

United Way

Many agencies receive support from the United Way. Once admitted, the agency receives funds each year. However, this is an extremely competitive source and new agencies are at a disadvantage since funds tend to go to well-established agencies. There is a donor option plan under which a donor can designate a specific agency to receive his gift. This should be investigated.

Adult Education and Community College

In many communities, teachers from Adult Education and the Community College are assigned to agencies to teach classes. A number of Art Centers for disabled people have taken advantage of this excellent service.

Graduate Students and Interns

Very often these students come to the Centers to do field work and gain practical experience. If they are well supervised and prepared, they are a valuable source of aid. They also help the Center maintain a normal environment.

Gifts in Lieu of Money

Very often state, city and county agencies, corporations and individuals are anxious to help but cannot provide the money. They may be willing to give gifts of furniture, equipment, and supplies which may be worth hundreds of dollars. They may even provide a building rent-free.

Corporate Consultation and Services

Some corporations may not supply money but are willing to send their expert staff as consultants to the Center or may be willing to train Center personnel. Such consultation may include accounting, fund raising, planning, and management. They may provide free services, such as printing, mailing, and volunteer workers. They may also provide members for the Board.

Volunteers

Volunteers provide a much-needed source of help to the Center. They can help in so many ways in fund-raising events, in solicitations, and in forming a bond with the community. They should be given recognition for the hours they serve without pay and must be given definite jobs. Volunteers should be made to feel needed and wanted.

Although these bits and pieces of funding may seem insignificant when taken alone, these contributions when added together may come to quite a sizeable amount. Another advantage is that the Art Center is constantly placed before the public eye. The greater the involvement of people, agencies and organizations, the more personal interest in the success of the undertaking, the more chance the Center will become a permanent asset to the community.

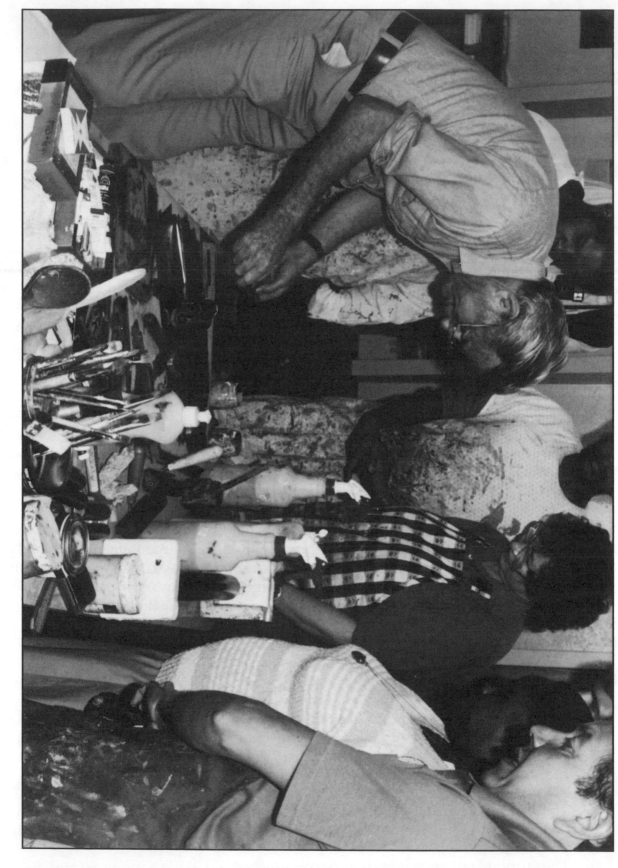

PROFESSOR KARL KASTEN OF U.C. BERKELEY DEMONSTRATES PRINT TECHNIQUES TO ARTISTS OF NATIONAL INSTITUTE OF ART & DISABILITES

14 The Art Center and the Art Community

The Director and the Board of Directors must understand the significant role that an Art Center for people with disabilities plays when it involves the entire art community.

What is the Art Community?

The art community consists of those who engage in or support the arts, either in a vocational or avocational manner. These include:

- Art museums, art galleries, community art centers and their auxiliaries, and other places that exhibit and/or sell art
- Artists
- Local and state art organizations
- State and local arts councils, the National Endowment for the Arts, Very Special Arts/ USA
- Organizations of artists with disabilities
- Art departments of universities, colleges, and high schools
- Art teachers
- Art newspapers, art magazines, art critics and writers
- Corporations, foundations, private organizations, and businesses interested in fostering the arts

The Art Center and Art Museums, Art Galleries, Community Art Centers

It benefits both the Art Center and these organizations if a close relationship between them is established. They have much in common. All are dedicated to making art a central force in people's lives, expanding public awareness, and carrying on educational programs in the arts. Having members who represent these other organizations on the Board of the Art Center and having a member who represents the Art Center on the Boards of other organizations solidifies this bond.

Benefits to the Art Center

- Exhibits of the great art of all ages act as excellent stimulation, learning, and resource material for the students and staff of the Art Center.
- Connection with these organizations gives the Art Center credibility in the art field.
- The Art Center should exhibit its artists' finest work in these established facilities. Individual artists of the Art Center should enter both juried and nonjuried shows.
- The Art Center should prepare and show educational exhibits on art and disabilities.
- The Art Center can educate the staff and docents of these organizations by familiarizing them with disabling conditions and making them aware of the creativity of disabled people.
- These organizations might sponsor conferences and workshops on art and disabilities.
- The Art Center can act as a consultant in preparing special exhibits appealing to the

disabled population.
o   Nondisabled artists have the opportunity of exhibiting their work in the Gallery of the Art Center.
o   Local art organizations can help support the Art Center.

Benefits to Art Organizations
o   The art organizations gain a totally new constituency of disabled people, particularly if the proper environment is established.
o   Staff skills are broadened to include awareness of disabilities. Staff members learn how to make disabled people psychologically and physically comfortable. Docents are trained to respect people with disabilities.
o   The organizations become more responsive to the needs of people with disabilities by ensuring handicapped access to the facility and by mounting, labelling, and lighting of exhibits.
o   Museums and galleries realize the need for exhibits appealing to people with special needs—touch exhibits and galleries primarily for the blind, lowered cases for wheel-chair viewing, exhibits of the work of famous artists with disabilities.
o   Galleries are enriched by exhibiting the work of people attending the Art Center.
o   Organiztions strengthen their position in the community by sponsoring conferences and workshops by and for people with disabilities.

The Art Center and Individual Artists, Local and State Art Organizations

Many artists are extremely sensitive to artists with disabilities. They appreciate the creativity and beauty of their art. They recognize the thin line that separates the able person and the disabled person.

Nondisabled artists can interact with the Art Center in varied ways. They can teach at the Art Center, exhibit their own work, take the work of disabled artists back to their own students for exhibition. A nondisabled artist may wish to take a artist with a disability as an apprentice. The nondisabled artist may wish to participate in fund-raising, teaching or demonstration lectures.

Virtually every community has some sort of association of artists. Many have their own gallery, meet regularly, issue newsletters, and install exhibitions. The Art Center should become an active participant and member in these groups.

In small communities, the local art organizations may not be as active as the state art organizations. By joining the state art organization, the Art Center can keep abreast of state/national events. They are in touch with the latest art events in the country and very often serve as an impetus to the community. It is beneficial to have a membership and keep in contact with the state organization.

The Art Center and the State Arts Council, National Endowment for the Arts, Very Special Arts/USA

The Art Center should also become involved in the State Art Council. Each State Council issues newsletters which provide current information about exhibits, art projects, recent developments in the art world, and announcements of grants and awards. The Art Council can also be approached by the Art Center as a source of funding. Different states vary in how actively the State Council participates in the local art community. Some of them have strongly supported art programming for the disabled community.

For many years, the National Endowment for the Arts has demonstrated interest in art and disabilities. The Endowment's Office of Special Constituencies serves as an advocate for programs aimed at disabled persons and other special groups. Endowment grants have supported special projects such as the following:

- o Establishing an art gallery showing the work of disabled artists
- o Funds to conduct training workshops for artists in residence, special education teachers, and administrators
- o Supporting artists in residence in Art Centers for people with disabilities
- o Supporting special art exhibits of work by disabled artists for circulation to different museums and galleries

Very Special Arts/USA, an educational affiliate of the John F. Kennedy Center for the Performing Arts, Washington, DC, has, since its inception, been a vital force in the recognition of art by disabled people. Its major function in the past has been to sponsor Very Special Arts Festivals in all art fields among disabled school children throughout the United States. It has also sponsored special projects involving both adults and children, including national art exhibits, dance and theater performances, publications, etc. Recently has changed direction somewhat, and is developing international programs and decentralizing so that each state will have more autonomy in developing its own Very Special Arts program.

As the work of artists with disabilities gains more acceptance in the art world, there is reason to believe that greater support will be provided at the national level.

The Art Center and Art Departments of Universities, Community Colleges, and High Schools

Art Centers should establish ties with art departments of educational institutions.

Benefits to the Art Center
- o Many of the teachers will become interested in the work of the Art Center and will recommend that their students visit the Art Center. These students can learn about the vital part disabled people can play in the arts, and the value of the Art Center.
- o Some students will become volunteers to help in the Art Center.
- o Some students, especially graduate students, will do projects with the Art Center— murals, banners, stained glass.
- o Students can form an auxiliary to help the Art Center on outings or in raising money.

Benefits to Educational Programs
- o Students will learn about the creativity of disabled people.
- o Students acquire a well-organized and exciting site to do field work and internships.
- o New vocations are opened to art students—director, teacher, curator.
- o Art students gain inspiration from the exciting art produced in the Art Center.

The Art Center and Art Publications

The Art Center should prepare illustrated articles for publication in art magazines and in art sections of newspapers and popular journals. Art critics should be invited to all exhibitions and their criticisms and suggestions should be welcomed.

Good publicity can profoundly influence the way the general public views the Art Center. Publicity can assist in fundraising from new sources, new volunteers, etc.

Published materials should be clipped and reproduced. These can be used when applying for grants and public support.

The Art Center and Corporations, Foundations, Private Organizations, and Businesses

Many foundations and organizations are especially interested in the arts. They feel pride in sponsoring worthwhile new endeavors. Very often, there are people on their Board or staff who are well acquainted with disabilities through family situations. To these people, the Art Center may be a particularly exciting field of interest for their support. It is important to make contact with these people and have them visit the Art Center so they will realize the vital art produced in these environments.

It is essential that the Art Center develop close relations with all segments of the art community and endeavor to become a vital force in the art community. When this happens the general public and the private sector will continue to support the Art Center both in its goals and its financial needs.

PUBLIC RELATIONS AND ADVOCACY

In order for the Art Center to grow it must be considered a valuable asset to the community. News about the Art Center should constantly reach the public. The Director, the staff, and the Board of Directors must take the time and energy to establish good relationships with social agencies, art groups, artists, other professionals, parents, other care facilities, politicians, disabled persons, volunteer organizations, business establishments, etc.

The Board of Directors, with its broad representation in the community, has an important role to play in the dissemination of any new and important developments occuring in the Art Center. Since the Art Center is such a new concept, it is in the forefront of discovery of new potentials of disabled people, thus helping to change stereotypes.

Together the entire staff, volunteers, the Director, and the Board are responsible for publicizing the Art Center and advocating for disabled people. There are many ways to do this. In our experience, the following have proven effective.

Press Releases

When significant news items occur, press releases should be prepared and sent to newspapers, TV and radio stations, magazines, and appropriate organization newsletters. Illustrative material, such as glossy photographs and/or art work will generally make the news items more attractive and more likely to be printed.

Workshops and Conferences

The Director and staff may wish to show interested individuals and groups what it feels like to be a participant in the Art Center's program.

A day can be set aside in the Art Center when invited guests can experience the activities at first hand and can learn through lectures, films, and slides. Workshops can be held for teachers, students, parents, etc.

Conferences on different aspects of art and disabilities can be held in the Art Center or in other appropriate places, such as museums, galleries, universities, theaters, etc.

Broadcasts (TV)

o Interviews with staff and students displaying and discussing student work
o A day at the Art Center showing students at work
o Special events taking place at the Art Center, such as an art sale of student work, students painting a mural, students working on a book or calendar, etc.
o Special events taking place outside the Art Center, such as a museum visit, a trip to an artist's studio, painting an outdoor mural, etc.

Broadcasts (Radio)

o Interviews with the Director and staff explaining philosophy and methods of working
o Interviews explaining changes of staff attitude in working with disabled artists/ students
o Interviews with visitors
o Interviews with students
o Questions and answers about the Art Center
o Announcements of special events

Exhibits

Dignified, professionally mounted exhibits should be placed in the Art Center's gallery, professional galleries, galleries in univerities and colleges, government buildings (courthouses, federal, state, county and city halls), libraries, and other appropriate spaces such as banks, protected shopping malls, theater lobbies, lobbies of large corporations, and department store windows. Exhibits should also be prepared for specific occasions and special events.

The Art Center's gallery can generate publicity. Newspaper, television and radio personnel are always looking for good stories and photographs. What a heyday for publicity when these people are moved by what they see!

Open House

Although the Art Center should never be closed to visitors, it can become disturbing to students if too many visitors come at one time. One alternative is to occasionally hold "Open House." This allows large numbers of visitors to be escorted around the Art Center and have the program explained to them. Students can be trained to conduct the tours, and have the opportunity to demonstrate their pride the Art Center and in their ability as artists and guides.

The Director and staff may wish to show interested individuals and groups what it feels like to participate in the Art Center's program. Special "Open Houses" can be arranged so that invited guests can experience the activities at first hand and learn through lectures, films, and slides.

Exchange Visits with Other Programs

The Director and staff members should cement relationships by exchanging visits with other relevant programs—in the neighborhood and elsewhere—thereby leading to a better understanding of mutual problems and concerns. Invitations to visit the Art Center should be extended to staff and students of other programs. Students and staff have much to gain by extending their horizons through mutual visits.

Calendars

An interesting way to share the Art Center's work with the community is to publish an widely-distributed calendar. To make this feasible, have a local organization or individual sponsor each page. This allows the cost of publishing to be spread across different members of the community while also involving them in the success of the Art Center. Students who illustrate the calendar have the pride of seeing their art published and appreciated by many people.

Students Illustrating Projects for Other Organizations

An excellent means to establish good relations between the Art Center and other organizations in the community is to have students illustrate the pamphlets, posters, newsletters, holiday cards, etc. for those organizations.

It is best if the student receives a fee for his work, and it is essential that the artist sign his work and the Art Center is appropriately acknowledged.

Posters, Cover Designs, Etc.

In much the same way, the students of the Art Center can design posters publicizing the Art Center, special events such as art exhibits, flea markets, Holiday sales, etc.

Publications

There is an enormous range of publications—from flyers to books. All of these might include illustrations by Art Center students. It is essential that these illustrations be of professional quality and that the artist and Art Center be acknowledged.

Every Art Center should have its own brochure.

Articles about the Art Center, about special events, and about the students should be published in journals, magazines, newspapers.

Reprints of newspaper and magazine articles about the Art Center and its students should be prepared for wide distribution.

Monographs can be issued on special topics, e.g., the work of individual students, the art of Down Syndrome artists, proceedings of workshops and conferences, etc.

Newsletters presenting events, plans, special contributions, memberships, honors to students/staff/Board members should be circulated.

Leaflets should advertise events and explain Art Center needs and accomplishments.

Very Special Art Festivals

For a number of years, Very Special Arts/USA (formerly the National Committee—Arts for the Handicapped) has sponsored Very Special Art Festivals which have greatly expanded public awareness of the importance of art in the lives of disabled people. These festivals usually consist of varied participatory art experiences: demonstrations and exhibits of art work by disabled children and adults. The VSAF movement is a powerful force in establishing and strengthening art programs for disabled people.

Disabled Artists Month/Week/Day

In order to involve broad segments of the community in understanding and appreciating the art of disabled people, a month, week, or day should be set aside each year to publicize their accomplishments. Museums and other public buildings can exhibit the art. Masks, costumes, and stage sets for special performances can be designed by Art Center participants. Television and radio programs can be encouraged to showcase the art of disabled persons. In addition, these activities are opportunities to involve artists who are not disabled.

Advocacy

It is a slow and difficult process to change people's attitudes about people with disabilities. However, by making the artistic accomplishments of disabled persons available for viewing, the general public will in time realize that disabled people are a positive force and have much to contribute and share with the rest of society.

15 The Staff of the Art Center

THE DIRECTOR'S DUTIES

The Director is responsible for carrying out the philosophy and policies formulated by the Board and must work closely with the Board at all times—especially during the early stages when the whole program of the Art Center is in a state of development. Most important, the Director must be in total agreement with the philosophy espoused by the Board.

The success of the fledgling Art Center depends largely on the leadership, ingenuity, dedication, knowledge, and understanding of the Director. He must be able to deal with the Board, the community, the students, the staff, and the immediate and long-term problems which are bound to arise.

The tone of the Art Center is set by the Director. His leadership can make it inspirational or mundane. Staff members are likely to take their lead from the Director and, together, the Director and staff have a profound impact on students, volunteers, visitors, parents, caretakers, and all others who interact with the Art Center.

The Director should be a practicing artist with an MFA degree or its equivalent. Only when a person himself engages in the creative arts can he have full empathy with the creative arts process. He should have successful administrative experience. Preferably he should have worked with people with disabilities and have knowledge of the service delivery system for people with disabilities. He must be convinced of their creative potentials of people with disabilities and must be dedicated to bringing out these potentials.

The job description for the position of Director should be clearly stated before the search begins. The position should be advertised widely in college and university art and education departments, art organizations, art magazines, and by word of mouth. Applicants should be sought from the disabled population and the group originally working toward the establishment of the Art Center. However, under no circumstances should the qualifications for this critical position be lowered to accommodate political or personal reasons. The best person available for the job is the *only choice*.

As soon as candidates for the position are identified, they should be interviewed by the Board. The Director should be hired for a specified probationary period—three to six months. Once the hiring takes place, the Director, working closely with the Board, becomes responsible for carrying out many specific tasks. Both the Board and the Director have many jobs in commmon. One of the most important and ongoing commitments is to establish the Art Center as an integral part of the community.

Performance must be reviewed by the Board prior to the end of the period. With the power of appointment comes the power of removal. If the Director is ineffectual or has too many problems due to lack of training, lack of experience, or personality, the Board should have no hesitancy in replacing this individual.

Hiring the Staff

The Director appoints the staff, provides supervision and inservice training. All employees should have a clearly defined job description approved by the Board of Directors. A probationary period is essential. Written evaluation by the Director must be made at least once a year. There should be no hesitancy about removing unsatisfactory employees.

The Director must encourage each employee to perform to his utmost capacity. Since disabled people have so many built-in limitations, it is necessary that the staff be of the highest quality to help students achieve to the best of their abilities.

The Director must be aware of the creative progress shown by each student. He must be able to help staff members understand changes in the students' work and the reasons for these changes. Are they due to teaching, to the studio environment, to home or outside influence, to the use of different art materials and techniques? He must be able to help the staff find means of alleviating problems which interfere with the students' ability to find their own methods in achieving quality work.

Setting Up the Space and Preparing the Facility for Use

It is assumed that the space has already been obtained by the Board of Directors. Since the quality of the environment is so important, one of the major jobs of the Director is to arrange the space in the most efficient and pleasant manner possible. Much will depend on his imagination and knowledge, available funds, the assistance of the community, of the staff, and of the private sector.

Selecting Art Experiences and Supplies

The Director is responsible for organizing the art experiences and obtaining the supplies. The art experiences will vary according to the philosophy, experience, and skills of the Director and the art teachers. The special needs of each student must be considered. The most appropriate art supplies must be obtained to carry on these art experiences.

Developing and Maintaining Records

The Director is responsible for organizing and maintaining a variety of records for the Center. Among the necessary records are financial records, memberships and contributions, historical records, legal records, mailing lists, employee and student records. Good record keeping is essential for efficient operation, for upgrading the quality of the program, and for accountability. It would be an excellent addition to have a computer for record keeping purposes.

Selecting Students

Since the population to be admitted has already been defined by the Board, it is the job of the Director to actively seek students for the program. It will be necessary to contact organizations and individuals who can identify and recruit disabled persons who are appropriate.

Publicizing the Center and Relating to the Community

No nonprofit organization can exist without community support. The Director must work closely with the Board of Directors in cultivating community interest. As the size of the Center increases, it may be beneficial to hire a publicity person. During the start-up period the job will fall upon the Director.

Fund Raising

The Director must be knowledgeable and, if possible, have had successful experience in fund raising. Much of this never ending responsibility will fall upon him. Certainly at the beginning, money will not be available to hire a specialized fund raiser. In cooperation with the Board of Directors, the Director must be able to write grant applications, solicit funds from individuals and corporations, and plan and carry out special fund raising events. Fund raising is an appropriate activity for the Director since he knows the organization, the students, the philosophy and is totally engrossed in the welfare of the organization.

Other Duties

- o   Preparing a brochure of the Center
- o   Preparing exhibits for the community and for travel
- o   Arranging art exhibits in the studio or gallery
- o   Preparing publications including newsletters
- o   Arranging special events
- o   Arranging cooperative ventures with schools
- o   Arranging for internships in the Center
- o   Arranging visits to the Center and greeting visitors
- o   Arranging student visits to artists' studios, to museums, and to other programs
- o   Planning conferences
- o   Attending meetings in related fields
- o   Meeting community leaders and politicians
- o   Arranging for lectures, films, tapes, radio and TV appearances

ART TEACHER(S)

As soon as money is available, an art teacher should be hired by the Director. A Director cannot teach and run the Center simultaneously. To teach art one must be completely engrossed in working with the students and not be bothered by constant interruptions.

Art teachers must be practicing artists, preferably with a Master of Fine Arts degree or its equivalent. If possible, the teacher should have had experience teaching people with disabilities. In any event, a teacher should be able to work without prejudice toward persons with intellectual, physical or emotional problems.

Since initially only one teacher will be hired, the teacher should have a wide variety to skills—painting, drawing, sculpture, printmaking, creative crafts. When the Art Center becomes large enough, each art teacher should be specialized in different art skills and interests.

In selecting an art teacher, the Director must examine the philosophy and ability of the applicant to establish and maintain a creative environment within the Center. The art teacher must believe that creativity lies within each person and that his job is to release this power. The teacher must present an open mind and must be genuinely excited by and appreciative of art that does not fit into any conventional style. He must be able to enjoy and appreciate primitive and unconventional art. He is there to help students fulfill their creative needs and must not impose his own preconceived ideas. He must allow each student to find his own style. This is doubly important since many persons with disabilities have long histories of being told what to do and how to do it. They have had limited opportunities for independent decision making and very often learn to be dependent on authority figures. It is easy for authority figures such as teachers to exert subtle or obvious influences which make their students dependent on them.

Since the teacher will be a creative person himself, he will be able to devise adaptations which will enable physically disabled students to resolve problems which will arise in using art materials.

A probationary period is essential for the teacher to test himself and be tested as to his feelings and abilities in working in this setting.

As soon as possible the art teacher must be indoctrinated by the Director as to the philosophy underlying the Center, the types of students entering the program, and the expectations of the Director as to quality standards.

The art teacher will work closely with the Director in making preparations for starting classes, setting up the studio area, selecting appropriate art activities, equipment and supplies, and preparing exhibits. Even before all preparations are complete, classes can begin.

When the studio population has grown large enough to employ two or three art teachers, a Head Art Teacher should be designated with a raise in pay commensurate with the added responsibility of supervision.

Duties of the Art Teacher

o   Stimulating the students
o   Providing art instruction as needed
o   Setting art goals for students
o   Reviewing students' progress
o   Keeping Director informed of students' progress in art and changes in their behavior
o   Keeping track of the art work and keeping a longitudinal art file for each student
o   Selecting art works for exhibit in the studio and for outside exhibits
o   Selecting and preparing art materials organizing clean-up of the studio
o   Keeping track of art supplies
o   Designing and using adaptations for physically disabled students

Attendant/Aide

If people with severe physical disabilities who need toileting assistance and other special care are admitted, an attendant is essential. The attendant must be skilled in lifting physically disabled people and should be able to feed and toilet them. The attendant will also prepare and distribute juices, coffee, fruit during break periods. If the students bring lunch, or if lunch is served at the Center, he should supervise this activity.

When the student group is small the attendant can be used as an assistant to the art teacher in straightening up shelves, giving out and putting away paper and supplies, etc.

Indoctrination to the program should be done by the Director and, if needed, by the art teacher. The attendant/aide serves a probationary period and is supervised by the Director or the Head Art Teacher.

Secretary

One of the first staff persons to be hired by the Director is a secretary. Since the operation will be small at this stage, the secretary must have many office skills. As the Director may be out of the Center a good deal of the time, the task of meeting visitors and explaining the program may fall on the secretary. The Director's first task is to indoctrinate him in the philosophy and operation of the program.

The secretary must not be prejudiced against persons with disabilities. He must be appreciative of the value of the arts in all people and especially in the lives of handicapped people. He must be able to serve as a receptionist, making students and visitors welcome and comfortable. Since there will be a great deal of paperwork, he must have good typing skills. He must be able to do elementary bookkeeping, filing and record keeping, and have a good presence on the telephone. He must also be able to keep track of and order all office supplies, and maintain the mailing list.

The secretary is under the supervision of the Director and serves a probationary period.

Accountant

An accountant, preferably a Certified Public Accountant, should be hired as soon as possible to oversee financial records and reports of the Center on a part-time or retainer basis. The credibility of the Center depends in part on its fiscal responsibility, especially in relation to fund raising and government assistance. Accurate and timely financial reports are essential to the proper management of the Center.

Social Worker/Counselor

Since the Art Center is an integral part of the network of community services for people with disabilities, it is essential to have at least one staff member responsible for relating to and communicating with social agencies, families, and caretakers. This person may be responsible for counseling students and helping them work out personal or social problems which keep them from fulfilling their creative potential. Since this person will know the disabled community, another aspect of his job will be to identify and recruit new students into the program.

Ideally, this person should be a licensed social worker or counselor experienced in working with handicapped persons, with a strong interest in the creative arts. Unless he believes in creativity and its worth to the person and to society, he cannot adequately fulfill his job.

Finding such a person is not as difficult as it may seem. There are many social workers who have had art training or who have a great appreciation and interest in art.

During the early months of the program, recruiting of students may have to be done by the Director. However, once the population reaches ten or more and there is sufficient income, a half-time social worker should be added to the staff. With 20 to 30 students, this position should be made full-time.

The social worker/counselor is supervised by the Director and serves a probationary period.

Other Positions

If money is available, other part-time or full-time positions would be advantageous:

Curator/Preparator. Since the Art Center at this stage is small and probably does not have its own gallery, a part-time person, either a teacher or a curator/preparator, is needed to curate and to prepare outside shows. This person mats, frames, prepares, arranges for, and hangs exhibits in the Center and in the community. He also keeps track of the exhibits and of the work exhibited and sold. He sends out press releases for each show, prepares interesting and unusual announcements and invitations and sends them to the Center's mailing list and to all interested persons and organizations. This position can be made full-time when the Center becomes financially able.

Photographer. Slides and photographs of students, their art work, the facility, and special events should be taken. The photographer should work with the Director and the curator/preparator in preparing special exhibits. At the early stage, this work may fall on the Director, teachers, or on volunteers.

Marketing Specialist. The marketing specialist aggressively merchandises and markets art produced by the artist-students. He makes contact with public agencies, nonprofit organizations, corporations and businesses such as retail and wholesale stores, to develop exhibitions and sales. This should be done in close collaboration with the Director and staff. The marketing specialist will also seek commissions which the students can carry out both in the Center and in the community.

Maintenance Person. Premises should be cleaned frequently. Students should help with cleanup after each day. When the Center can afford it, it should be cleaned professionally each evening.

Public Relations. A person experienced in preparing publicity would be of great advantage to the Center. Stories about the students, the faculty, art shows, Center activities, awards should be written and illustrated for specific publications. This person should keep in constant touch with radio, television, newspapers, popular and professional art as well as disability publications. He should prepare and be responsible for the distribution of the Center newsletter and publications.

Fund Raiser. A person who is familiar with public and private sources and is innovative in creating new ways of raising funds should be hired part-time or full-time when money is available.

1 6 Volunteers

Once the staff has been selected, it would be a great asset to establish a volunteer group. There are so many and varied ways in which organizations and individuals can help an Art Center for people with disabilities. Not only will the persons with disabilities benefit but the volunteers will have their lives enriched through the experience of volunteering. They are out in the community and should be invited to help from the very beginning. All volunteers should be made aware of the value of their contributions and the Center should not neglect to thank them.

Helping Locate and Preparing the Facility for Use

Volunteers can be of much help in locating a suitable space and preparing it for occupancy. Many have great skills in real esate, construction, electrical wiring, plumbing.

Service clubs are often helpful once they become convinced that the project is worthwhile. Among such clubs are Kiwanis, Rotary, American Association of University Women, Junior League, etc. A good example is the help of the Kiwanis Club in building ramps when the Institute was first established in Richmond.

Helping Establish a Normal Environment in the Studio

Individuals sit with the students, paint, sculpt, and do various art activities as peers. Students benefit by having excellent role models of behavior, dress, attitudes, work habits. Volunteers gain by having varied art experiences and forming friendships with people with whom they ordinarily would have no association.

Helping with Studio Chores

A volunteer can help mix paint, prepare clay, distribute paper, help dispense tools. The volunteer gains experience in learning many new skills. The teachers are relieved of many duties so they can spend more time in actual teaching. The student gains from greater interaction with nonhandicapped people.

Helping Prepare Students for Art Work

Many students with disabilities need help with taking off their coats, being helped in putting on smocks, being helped into their seats. Volunteers enjoy the contact with the students and the feeling of being needed.

Helping Prepare Students to Leave

Before the students leave for the day, many chores must be done. Paints must be collected, brushes washed, clay put away, tools cleaned. Also many students with severe disabilities must be helped to clean the tables and chairs, to wash up, to take off their smocks, to put on their coats, to be escorted to the door or to the bus. Teachers are always overextended at this time and volunteers will feel a real sense of being needed.

Helping Prepare and Distribute Snacks

Eating is a pleasant activity much enjoyed by the students. Snacks can be prepared and distributed at specified times. If the student stays all day, either he must bring his lunch or lunch must be prepared at the Center. In either case, volunteers can be of great help. They can also eat with the students, thus serving as role models. To share a sandwich or a piece of fruit can be the start of real friendship and understanding.

Helping with Travel Training

Volunteers can go to homes of individual students and train them to ride on public transportation to the Art Center. They also can return the student to his home on public transportation. The volunteer has the satisfaction of a rewarding experience and a sense of real accomplishment when the student learns to travel by himself. The freedom of being able to use public transportation opens a whole new world to the student.

Transporting Students to the Center

Students who are unable to learn to use public transportation can be taken in the volunteer's car to the Center. This would enable students to participate who could not otherwise be able to come to the Center.

Assisting Staff Members in Taking Students on Field Trips and Visits

There are many field trips and visits of educational and artistic value. Among these are visits to museums, galleries, theater performances, the opera, ballet, parks. This is a rewarding experience for volunteers since the visits are extremely enjoyable. This type of experience should only be done with very small numbers. It is not normal for large groups to be "walked through" such experiences.

Assisting Staff Members in Taking Students on Vacation or Recreational Expeditions for Art Stimulation

Trips can be arranged to Disneyland, Marine World, national and state parks. In Scandinavia, for example, every disabled person has a two-week vacation in Spain, England, or some foreign country. In our country short trips of one or two days can be managed with the help and cooperation of volunteers.

Providing Opportunties for Students to be with a Real Family

So many of the students have been hospitalized for so many years that they are alienated from normal living. Also they have lost contact with their families. They feel the need of belonging, of some person or family to be loving and caring. In the board and care homes in which most are presently living, there is a great variety of relationships. Unfortunately, most homes are concerned only with fulfilling bodily needs—a house (not a home) to live in, food for sustenance, and garments to cover the body. This does not answer the cravings of the human soul nor does it stimulate growth.

The feelings of abandonment and isolation are most strong during holiday seasons when families get together on Thanksgiving Day, Christmas, Easter, and on birthdays. Volunteers could do much if they invited a lonely disabled person to their homes for a special holiday dinner. Even a short visit does much to make a person feel wanted and appreciated. Very often a volunteer will pick one student and form this kind of bond through the years. The student will look forward to the times when he will be visiting with his "family" or "friend." It is hard to convey how much difference even one caring person makes to formerly "institutionalized" people.

Fund Raising Events—A Constant Need

Volunteers can raise money for the Center while engaging in activities they enjoy. Such activities can take many and diverse forms. Following is a partial list:
- Flea markets
- Parties in their own homes—such as Tupperware social parties, parties featuring political figures, fashion shows
- Raffles
- Bingo games
- Sports events

Only a person's imagination limits the ways he can raise money for a worthy organization.

Photography, Videotapes, Tapes, Motion Pictures

Volunteers can do much to document everyday happenings in the Center as well as to record special events such as parties, conferences, outings. The staff seldom has time to do this. Many of these pictures and tapes can also be used for publicity purposes.

When a photograph showing a student engaging in a special event is given to him it has a tremendous value. The look on the student's face, the joy of seeing himself is enough reward in itself.

Helping Conduct Recreational Activities

There are certain activities which would benefit the students greatly but which cannot be provided as integral parts of the Art Center. These could be carried on by volunteers especially interested in such activities, either after Center hours or on weekends. Among these activities are dancing, swimming, baseball, bowling, music. The volunteer could do this either with an individual student or a small group of students.

Helping Conduct Parties

All people love a party, especially those who are denied the pleasure. There could be wonderful party days when students dress up, dance, entertain and are entertained. Party food is enjoyed by all. Parties can be done on a monthly basis in honor of those having birthdays that month, or on holidays. These can be held in the Center or in other locations.

Basic Learning Experiences

Many students wish to learn to read, write, or do arithmetic. This can be taught one to one or in small groups. Many students would be willing to stay an extra hour once or twice a week to learn and to have the special attention given by volunteers.

Basic Independent Living Skills

Many students wish to learn these skills. These can be taught by using practical experiences related to their lives. Students could be taken shopping, using their money and counting their change. They could shop for and prepare snacks for the entire Center. How rich these experiences could be!

Setting Up and Operating a Library for Students

An art library for students serves many purposes. Among them are stimulation, normalization, and engaging in an adult activity. Books and magazines expand the students' horizons by bringing them the finest examples of the arts throughout history. Excellently illustrated books and magazines of interesting places could be introduced to the students. A person is needed to collect books, classify them, keep them in order. Since few students can read, profusely illustrated books are of tremendous importance. Volunteers could answer the students' questions and help them understand what they are looking at.

Taking Students to the Public Library

A volunteer could take either a small group or an individual student to the library once or twice a week. He would help them obtain a library card, pick out appropriate books, and teach them to use the library on their own.

Setting Up and Maintaining a Picture Library for Students in the Center

Pictures are used for stimulating the imagination. Such a library would contain photographs of paintings, sculpture, architecture, crafts, masks, costumes, nature, different cultures. The volunteer could obtain free pictures, mount them, classify them and keep them readily available.

Assisting the Curator

Volunteers can be trained as docents to explain the work of students to visitors to the gallery or to the program. They can help canvass the community for places to set up exhibits, make contact with those in charge of theaters, department stores, shopping malls, public builings, and arrange for exhibits in these places.

Student Auxiliary

High school and college fraternities should be encouraged to "adopt" the Center. When interested and moved, their energy and ideas know no bounds.

They can hold all sorts of events—sports events, parties, concerts, dances with the funds going to the Center for scholarships, supplies, and equipment.

Many are gifted and can help with student parties by playing music for student dances, by providing entertainment, by helping prepare and distribute the food, or just by being there as friends.

Another wonderful way to help is a fun day in the park with all the trimmings—picnic, ball games, swimming.

This is only a partial list of the infinite number of ways a volunteer can help the Art Center fulfill its commitment to people with disabilities. Each person who becomes a volunteer brings a message to the community of the worth and accomplishments of the organization. A loyal bond springs up between the volunteers and the Art Center.

17 Setting up the Space and Preparing the Facility for Use

The working space should be light, large, uncramped, giving the feeling of freedom, a place where people can work together or, if needed, by themselves. It need not be expensive or luxurious. It must be pleasant and stimulating to work in. It should be able to be made warm enough in winter and cool enough in summer so the work can be carried on comfortably regardless of season.

Ideally, the Art Center should have an exhibit space or art gallery where the students' work and the work of outside artists, both those with handicapping conditions and those without, can be shown. If this is not possible, wall space should be set aside for display of student work.

The facility should be accessible in several ways.

People with handicapping conditions should have no difficulties in negotiating all available spaces with complete safety. There should be no physical barriers anywhere—work areas, display areas, offices, toilets, or other parts of the facility.

The building should be easily accessible by public transportation, with students, staff and visitors able to come and go on their own as much as possible.

The space should be psychologically accessible, as a place where people will enjoy working and displaying their work. The neighborhood should not pose a threat to people with disabilities.

Remodeling

Most buildings will require some remodeling before they can be used. For example, there may be need for painting, for accessible toilets, ramps, sinks, walls, partitions, heating, electrical or roofing repairs. In some cases the landlord may be willing to remodel if there is a long-term lease. Since there is such variability in what remodeling costs may be, we have not included any specific figures. It is essential that estimates of these costs from reliable contractors be considered before the building is rented or purchased. These costs must be considered before the budget is prepared.

As little remodeling as possible to make the program operational should be undertaken when the Center is to pay the cost. Very often, when the program has proved its contribution to the community, funds for remodeling will be much more easy to obtain. Many companies, service clubs, or individuals will give free services, supplies, or contributions for specific needs—such as easily accessible toilets, efficient lighting, painting, ramps—when they can actually see a well-functioning program with specific needs. Also, government funds may be available for this purpose from the state, county, or city.

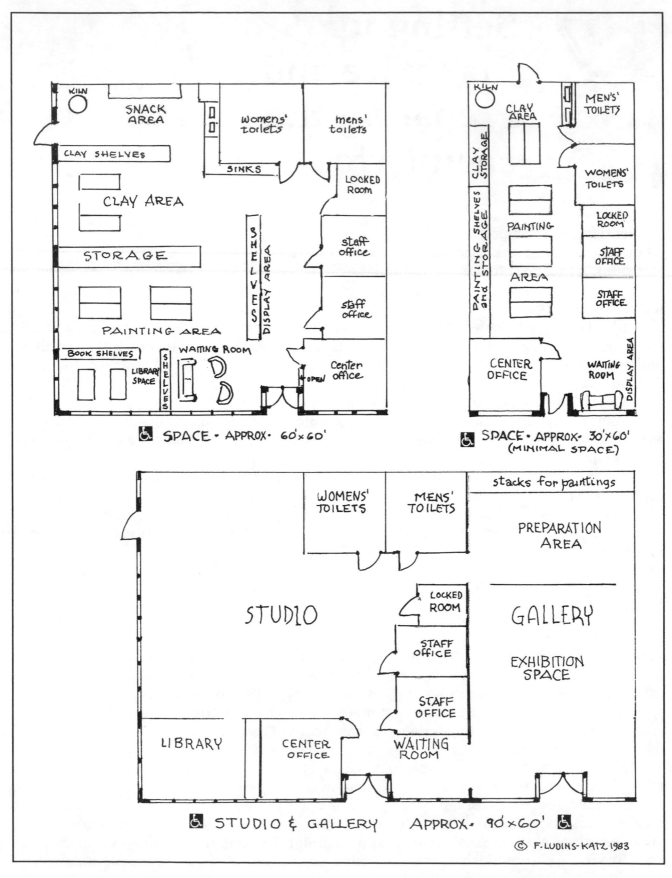

SPACE · APPROX · 60'×60'

SPACE · APPROX · 30'×60'
(MINIMAL SPACE)

STUDIO & GALLERY   APPROX · 90'×60'

© F. LUDINS-KATZ 1983

SUGGESTED FLOOR PLANS

Planning the Space

Once a site that meets the specifications has been selected, careful planning must be undertaken to prepare the facility for use. Consideration must be given to the number of students who will initially and eventually occupy the space, the number of students in wheelchairs, what art activities they will engage in, whether they will be eating lunch in the building, where students should hang their coats, where offices, storage space, toilet facilities, emergency and fire exits should be located. A space must be allocated as an emergency rest area. A kitchen with stove, sink, and refrigerator should be made available. There should be total accessibility to all spaces.

Scale floor plans should be prepared so that different arrangements can be studied. Despite all the preliminary planning, there will have to be a period of trial and error to find out what works best. Initially it is wise to maintain flexible spaces with easily movable partitions. The feeling of open space should be maintained. In planning and arranging the space, all staff members should be involved.

Free consultation often can be obtained from university departments of architecture, from corporations or from architectural firms. Some foundations offer space-planning grants. A Board member may have expertise in space planning. At this stage as much help as possible should be sought. It is much more efficient and less costly to plan well before preventable errors are made.

Studio Set-up

Each building will have to be studied to arrive at the best plan for use of the space. In setting up the space the studio work areas should not be overcrowded. Students and staff should have room to move about freely. There should be plenty of room for wheelchairs. It is wise to set up definite spaces for different art activities.

Consideration must be given to the nature of each different material. Clay by its very composition is messy. It can cause great grief if it is not kept separate from other activities. Paints must be kept away from the drawing tables, especially since many of the drawings will be used for illustrations and posters and must be kept clean. The wood sculpture is noisy and must be placed where hammering will be least disturbing to others. A kiln may emit hazardous fumes and this must be considered in planning.

Open shelves, closed cupboards, bins, and space for tools are necessary. Open shelves should be available for paper, brushes, paints, tools, and other supplies so that each student can easily get what he needs without being dependent on teachers. Closed cupboards are needed for valuable supplies, sharp tools, or for supplies that will be needed for future or designated use. Bins for clay and wood should also be easily accessible. Shelves for greenware, bisque, and glazed work must be set up. A special section should be set aside for sharp or electrical tools.

Sinks and counters for mixing paints, cleaning brushes, and clay tools must be of proper height and accessible to those in wheelchairs.

If possible, each student should be allocated a space where he can place his own special supplies, e.g., a specially adapted brush, a favorite pen, special ink, crayons.

Folding lunch room tables with formica tops are well suited for painting, drawing, and clay work. These can be easily cleaned with soap and water and can be folded up when the space is needed for other activities such as meetings, showing of films, dances. Chairs should be sturdy, easily cleaned, comfortable, and the proper height for the tables.

Equipment

The following items of equipment should be obtained as soon as possible since they will be in constant use from the start:

- o Paper cutter
- o Professional mat cutter
- o Clay wedging board
- o Woodworking bench
- o Two cameras, one Polaroid and one 35 mm
- o Projection screen
- o Slide and movie projectors
- o Photographic lights
- o Drying racks for finished paintings

If funds are available, a kiln, an etching press, a 16 mm movie camera, a xerox machine, and a computer would be great assets from the very beginning. A washing machine and dryer for student smocks will save much time. The smocks worn by the students must be constantly washed since many of the students are unable to keep themselves clean. Of course a laundromat may be used if no money for this equipment is available, but it is much less efficient and more costly in the long run than having the machines in the Center. However, these are expensive items and their purchase should be delayed rather than buying cheap machines. A dishwasher is an excellent addition that helps prevent the spread of colds.

Specialized Equipment (see Appendix A)

A person with a disability who ordinarily cannot function as an artist may be able to do so if specialized equipment is made or adapted for his use. Tables of special heights may have to be designed and constructed to accommodate people in wheelchairs or people with particular physical disabilities. Chairs may have to be modified for people with orthopedic problems.

Although table top and floor easels can be purchased, specially constructed ones are sturdier and better suited for individual needs.

Brushes, pens, pencils and chalk can be easily adapted for use by people who have great difficulty in grasping and holding.

Paint pans can be invented to meet specific needs.

Free and Low Cost Equipment and Furniture

Large corporations, banks, colleges, schools, government agencies often have warehouses in which they store surplus chairs, tables, desks, filing cabinets, shelves, xerox machines, typewriters, stoves, sinks, washing machines, and other odds and ends. These may not be beautiful or fashionable but usually are sturdy and with a little fixing and painting can be used when starting a program. It may take a long time before the Art Center is able to purchase furniture and equipment which it is proud to own.

By getting furniture and equipment free, money can be used for more specialized necessities such as screens for hanging paintings, drying racks, a kiln, an art press, a professional mat cutter, frames.

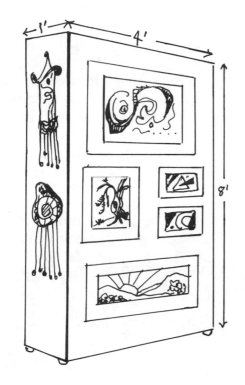

Materials

    2 - 4' x 8' sheets of 1/2" or 3/4"
      plywood
    2 - 1' x 8' pieces of plywood
    2 - 1' x 4' pieces of plywood
    4 wheels

    Display panels can be covered with
burlap or monk's cloth and/or painted.
    One sheet of 4' x 8' plywood can
be eliminated and shelves for pottery
or sculpture can be substituted. One
side still remains to display paintings.

Materials

    3 hollow core doors
    2 sets of hinges with
      removable pins

    Both sides can be
used for display.
    Panels can be
easily separated for
handling, storage and
shipping.

© F. LUDINS-KATZ 1983

DISPLAY PANELS

Exhibition Space

If it is possible, a professional gallery space in or close to the studio should be included. There are many reasons for providing such a display area. The beauty, expressiveness, and high quality of art work produced by many disabled persons is worthy of exhibit for its artistic merit. There is tremendous pride in seeing one's work valued and deserving of being shown to the public in a professional environment. Even at an early stage in the development of the Art Center, it is important for the public and professionals to learn to appreciate the quality and expressiveness of the art work, thereby changing the stereotypes of people with disabilities.

Exhibits provide a place where work can be sold, or where organizations can obtain or rent the art work for display in other settings. Newspapers and magazines as well as art associations and galleries can be invited to see the art work.

If it is not possible to have a professional gallery, space within the studio itself must be set aside for exhibits. This can be accomplished by having walls especially designated for this purpose or by constructing special display panels.

STORAGE OF ART WORK

Since the collection and preservation of art work is an important function of the Art Center, storage space for finished work should be provided from the beginning.

Paintings and Prints. A system must be devised to keep paintings by each student in chronological sequence. Portfolios are an excellent method. They must be easily accessible for viewing by students, staff, and visitors. Racks are an efficient method of storing portfolios. Small drawings, paintings and prints can be preserved by placing them in filing cabinets.

Matted, mounted or framed paintings suitable for sale should be placed on racks which are easily accessible. All paintings and racks should be clearly labeled.

Murals. Storage of murals is difficult. Their size and fragility may require them to be rolled and not opened frequently. It is recommended that slides and photographs be made to minimize the necessity of handling the originals.

Sculpture. Ceramic, paper and wood sculpture are also difficult to store because of their bulk and fragility. If possible all should be photographed and a record maintained. The best should be kept and stored on shelves.

Permanent Collection. It is important for an Art Center to have a permanent collection of the finest work students produce. All such work should be clearly labelled as belonging to the permanent collection. A permanent collection should also be kept of sequences of art work, showing the progress of a particular student. The permanent collection should be exhibited, but not sold. Every effort should be made to keep the art from deterioration.

Food Preparation and Eating Space

If students are to remain a full day, space must be set aside for lunch. A refrigerator and stove, a kitchen sink, cupboards, and a place to store food and utensils will be needed. If money is available, a dishwasher is an extremely welcome addition.

Even if students come part-day, a snack space will be needed. This space is also important

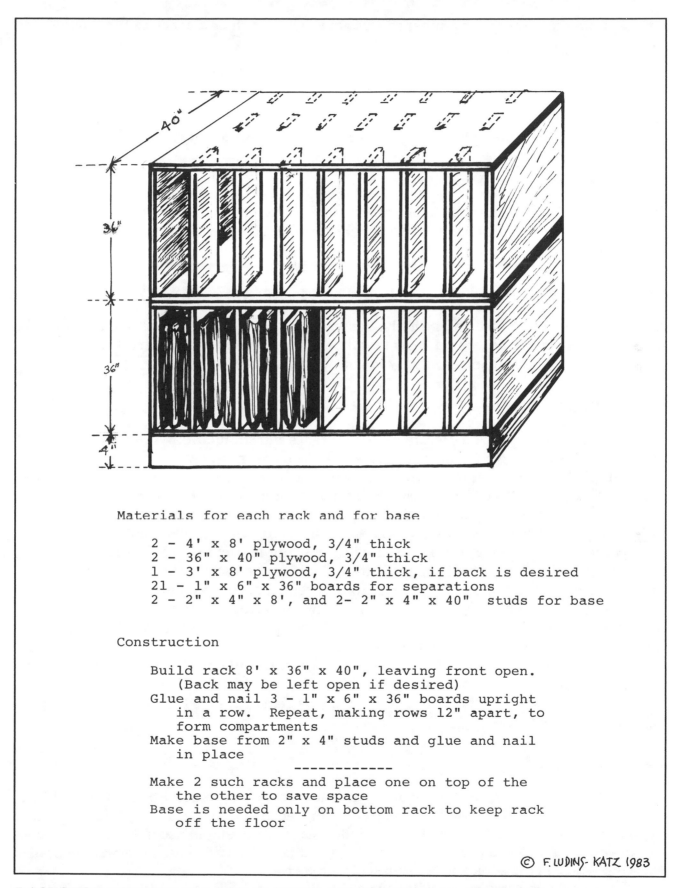

Materials for each rack and for base

    2 - 4' x 8' plywood, 3/4" thick
    2 - 36" x 40" plywood, 3/4" thick
    1 - 3' x 8' plywood, 3/4" thick, if back is desired
    21 - 1" x 6" x 36" boards for separations
    2 - 2" x 4" x 8', and 2- 2" x 4" x 40" studs for base

Construction

    Build rack 8' x 36" x 40", leaving front open.
        (Back may be left open if desired)
    Glue and nail 3 - 1" x 6" x 36" boards upright
        in a row. Repeat, making rows 12" apart, to
        form compartments
    Make base from 2" x 4" studs and glue and nail
        in place

    Make 2 such racks and place one on top of the
        the other to save space
    Base is needed only on bottom rack to keep rack
        off the floor

© F. LUDINS- KATZ 1983

RACKS FOR PORTFOLIOS AND MATTED OR FRAMED PAINTINGS

for hospitality to visitors. If no other space is available, lunch or a snack can be eaten in the studio.

Toilets

All equipment and accessories (towel racks, mirrors, sinks, toilets) should be fully accessible to people in wheelchairs so they can manage their own needs as much as possible.

Office Space

Offices of the Director, the counselor, secretary, and other personnel should be placed so the students have easy access to all the personnel with whom they work. Temporary screens can be used for partitions.

Library Space

A library is an excellent advantage to the Center but is not a necessity. Much thought must be given to where it will be located, how it will be used, who will use it, what material it is to contain, how it will be financed, and who will supervise its use.

Picture File for Students

It is a good idea to organize a picture file for reference and stimulation. A person must be put in charge who will organize the pictures and keep them in order. The file should contain excellent photographs of animals, flowers, trees, seascapes, cities, houses. Different cultures should be represented such as African, Eskimo, American Indian, East Indian, Oriental. The collection should contain photographs of outstanding works of contemporary art and art of past eras. This collection can easily be classified and stored in a file cabinet.

These photographs are to be used as stimulating and enriching experiences—*not as material to be copied*. For example, if a student is painting a forest scene, at some point the teacher may find it advisable to show him photographs of trees, flowers, foliage and animals that exist in such an environment. This adds a whole new dimension to the student's visual vocabulary. It does not necessarily mean that the student will incorporate these into his picture. It will be up to the student to use or not to use this material.

Public libraries will usually donate old magazines containing excellent photographs. Stores and especially museum stores have wonderful pictorial calendars. Since the time for selling the calendars is so short, they will usually be glad to donate them as soon as the sales season for the item ends.

Book Library

It is important to start a library as soon as possible. Ideally a trained librarian should be in charge but this is rarely possible. Perhaps a volunteer can be found. In any circumstance, a person must bve placed in charge and a definite area must be established if it is to work. Books disappear when records are not kept. Therefore, it is necessary to set up a written system showing who has the book and when it will be returned.

Books are necessary in the following fields:

For the teacher
- o   Art techniques - painting, printmaking, sculpture, weaving
- o   Art teaching and student development
- o   Teaching of students with special needs
- o   Special projects in art
- o   Informational books on different aspects of disabilities
- o   Art history - Contemporary, primitive, naive, classic

For the student
- o   Art books containing photographs of both contemporary art and art of other eras
- o   Art books of individual artists and craftsmen
- o   Beautifully illustrated books (very often children's books)
- o   Books with excellent photographs of nature, people, places, and objects
- o   Art and nature magazines

Audio-Visual Library

This necessitates a secure storage area, a person in charge, a place for showing, and projection equipment.

An area should be capable of being darkened so that slides and films can be shown to students, staff, or visitors.

Many of these components of an Art Center will not be feasible at the beginning. Every effort should be made to interest the community in procuring these items and facilities. If you can catch people's or an organization's imagination, very often they will be the catalyst that makes things happen.

18 Admitting Students

Referrals of disabled persons to the Art Center will come from a variety of sources: parents, board and care home operators, social workers, social agencies, public and private schools, psychologists, psychiatrists, physicians, mental health professionals, self-referrals, and from media coverage.

Suitable students will fall into two main groups: those who are talented in the visual arts and those who wish to try working in the visual arts although they may not have had any art experience.

Since creating art is a developmental process, it is not always possible to know those who are gifted until they have had ample time to work in the arts. However, given the opportunity and the encouragement, the discovery of those who are gifted is an exciting and triumphal experience both for them and for the staff. Those who come to the Center acclaimed as "artistic" may be far outstripped by student who have never had the opportunity to use art as a creative medium. Even when the person does not progress rapidly, the opportunity to develop his creativity should be provided. A person should never be denied access to the program because of an apparent lack of ability. It is much more important that this should be a growing and enjoyable experience.

Only when a student has tried being in the program and finds that he does not wish to continue, should he be dropped.

The Director and social worker must actively seek potential students who are particularly suited for this program. This may require visits to social agencies, visits to schools graduating potential students, meetings with parents, professionals, and friends of disabled persons, writing articles for newspapers and magazines, explaining the program on television and radio, and showing student art in many places.

Students should be admitted one at a time, if possible. Each must be looked upon as an individual and as a total person. Time must be allowed for him to observe the program and for the staff to learn his idiosyncracies and strengths. This cannot be done when a large group of new students makes a sudden appearance, overwhelming and confusing the staff and other students.

Procedure for Admission

When a person has been referred as a potential student various steps are set in motion.

The person and his guardian and/or social worker are invited to visit the Center. At the initial visit the prospective student and those who accompany him are interviewed by the Director and/or the social worker. Whenever possible the student should be asked questions directly. If he is not able to express himself verbally, the person who accompanies him provides basic information, including emergency phone number and person to contact. The prospective student is then shown around the Center, introduced to the staff and students, and invited to participate in an art activity with other students.

If the person indicates that he enjoys himself and wants to be in the program, arrangements are made for a trial period of three months. Transportation and fee arrangements will have to be worked out before admission.

If the student definitely does not wish to come, no further arrangements are made at this time.

It is very hard to judge from the first visit. A number of students who seem to show little interest during the initial visit have later indicated they wish to return and have been admitted. It must be realized that many disabled people have never had an opportunity to engage in an art experience. Prospective students must be given opportunities to acclimate themselve to a totally new environment and may need to return a few times before they are comfortable.

During the trial period complete information should be obtained about the student's personal, social, educational, and medical background. Necessary releases and waivers will have to be completed. (See Appendix D.)

Rejection or exclusion from the program should be based *only* on lack of interest, lack of desire to continue, destructiveness to the environment, to persons working in the Center, or to oneself. If no attendant is available, an otherwise possible candidate may have to be rejected because he cannot take care of his physical needs.

It is suggested that, under ideal circumstances, the population be increased slowly. During the first month no more than five students should be admitted. During the second month the total population can be increased to ten. An admission rate of no more than five persons per month seems reasonable until the planned maximum has been reached. There must be time to study each person and to give a newcomer individual attention.

19 Records

Since there are so many records to be kept, a computer would be of great advantage from the inception of the Center.

CENTER RECORDS

Financial Records

Financial records must be kept for ongoing monitoring by the Director, for tax purposes, for accountability to various government agencies, for credibility to funding sources, and for the Board of Directors. It is essential that an appropriate and efficient accounting system of recording income and expenditures be established under the direction of a professional accountant. A large corporation may be willing to assist in this task, for which a tax write-off may be taken.

Employee Records

Files must be maintained for all employees, consisting of resume of background and experience, health, salary, attendance, annual evaluations by supervisor, and any special honors or special reports.

Volunteer and Intern Records

Records should be kept of names, addresses, company affiliations, days and hours of work. Frequently this information is needed when applying for jobs. Evaluations should also be kept on record.

Memberships, Contributions

Records of the names, addresses, amount of contribution, and date should be kept of members and donors. Records of in-kind contributions are essential.

Grants from Government Agencies, Foundations, and Corporations

A separate file should be kept of each grant, containing all letters and notations of phone calls, meetings, visits, names of contact people, evaluation, and outcome.

Historical Records

A Center should establish and maintain a historical file which records the growth of the Center, with written and photographic documents, all newspaper and magazine articles, publications, press releases, circulars of special events, and any publications concerning these events and other pertinent information.

Legal Records

The Articles of Incorporation and Bylaws should be available at all times and should be updated. The names, addresses, occupation, business address, and phone number of all Board members should be on file. There should be a complete file of all minutes of the meetings of the Board of Directors and resolutions and actions of the Board. Federal, state, county or city licenses and Center contracts should be on file.

Correspondence Files

All pertinent correspondence should be filed and made accessible.

Mailing Lists

A comprehensive updated mailing list with addresses and telephone numbers of members, visitors, volunteers, interns, persons and organizations who have made inquiries, persons who have purchased student work or Center publications, who have made donations of money, materials or labor, people interested in arts and disabilities, museums and art galleries, newspapers, magazines, and local television and radio stations should be maintained. Such a list is essential for fund solicitation, events, newsletters, and for emergency meetings and announcements.

ARTIST-STUDENTS' RECORDS

There are two types of records necessary for each student—art records and personal records.

Art Records

Portfolio of Paintings, Prints and Drawings. Each student should have a portfolio of his own bearing his name and containing all significant paintings, prints and drawings. The work should be kept in chronological order with each dated and signed. Small works often get lost or messed up in a large portfolio. It is best to keep these in a file cabinet with each artist's work in a separate folder bearing the name of the artist.

At the beginning all art should be kept. But since some people are so prolific, before long it will prove impossible to keep everything. When work is to be eliminated, careful choices must be made not to discard quality work just because of quantity. In order not to distort the record of the process of growth of the individual the following procedures are suggested:

o   Keep all examples of an artist-student's first few weeks' work.
o   Keep all the best works.
o   Keep any works which show difference or change, whether for the better or for the worse.
o   An entry should be made on the portfolio of the date the selection and elimination is made, the number of pieces eliminated, and the name of the person or persons doing the selecting.
o   The artist should participate in this selection process if possible.

The portfolio is one of the most important records of the artist-student's creative growth and is an invaluable evaluation tool. It shows what he was capable of doing when admitted, the time he took to develop, the stages of development, and his total growth during the program. It is often amazing, even for those who have been with the student from the initial phases, to review the portfolio and recapture the early days of the student's work and to retrace the development through the years. It is also of tremendous significance for the student to realize his own growth. The student's work should be reviewed with him periodically.

Three-dimensional Art Work and Murals. Sculpture of clay, wood or paper, mosaics of stone, ceramics, glass or wood, weaving made with natural objects and wool, assemblages of wood, paper, metal, and large murals are most difficult to store in the Center because of size, weight, fragility, and inadequate storage space. The best pieces must always be kept but the great majority will have to be taken home by the students. It is absolutely essential that slides be taken or photographs be made before these pieces are taken from the studio. These slides and photographs, together with the actual pieces, serve the same purpose as the portfolio in tracing the progress of the student.

For parents, caretakers, teachers, professional workers, and researchers, the portfolio and the three-dimensional collection represent the most potent signs of growth in the student. The collection is significant for interns and for those who are learning about art and disabilities. It is an endless resource for research in this field.

Slide and Photographic Collection of Student Work. Ideally, a slide or photograph should be made of every piece of work by the student. However, this is an impossible task. The selection of works to be photographed will depend entirely on the orientation and interests of the Director and staff. Slides and photographs are easy to store, take little space, and are easy to review. Each slide should have the student's name, date of completion, and medium. Very often galleries and museums ask to view slides when they are preparing art shows; they expect slides of professional photographic quality. Newspapers and magazines often ask for similar quality photographs.

Personal Records

For each student, the following records should be kept in an individual folder in a *locked* file. Confidential material should be released only with written permission. There should be complete background information on social, psychological, medical, educational, institutionalization, and other significant data. Incident reports of unusual happenings and behavior should be recorded by the staff. Records should be kept of student exhibitions, sales and publications, case review reports, Individual Program Plans (IPP), an entry report when the student is admitted, a final report when the student leaves the program, releases for photographs of the student and his work, releases for showing of art work, and releases to go on trips.

Case Reviews

Frequent case discussions among staff members are necessary in order to better understand each student, to set reasonable and meaningful goals, to evaluate creative progress, and to assess development in other areas.

Time for case reviews for each student should be regularly scheduled at least once in six months. All staff working with the student should actively participate in the discussion. Whenever possible, the students should be invited to these reviews. In some situations it may be preferable to have the student come for only part of the case reivew. Parents, caretakers, social workers, and representatives of other organizations working with the student should be invited whenever appropriate.

Typically, the case review includes a summary of the student's background, the place of the Center in the student's life pattern, development in art, changes in attitudes and behavior, reasons for these changes, and special incidents which have occurred. The portfolio and slides are reviewed and evaluated. Previously established goals are examined and new goals set. Methods to be used in accomplishing these goals are formulated.

Each case review should be recorded with date and names of persons participating. These reviews are confidential and should be kept in the student's folder in a locked file.

Additional Files

It is an excellent idea to keep files such as the following:
- o Sources of art materials - catalogues and price lists
- o Sources of free and inexpensive art materials
- o Sources of free and inexpensive equipment, furniture, supplies
- o Sources of free and inexpensive party materials - ice cream, cake, candy, wine, cheese, decorations
- o Picture files for students' use
- o Files of volunteers, professionals, and contractors
- o Files of grant applications
- o Files of disabled artists

Slides, Photographs, Videotapes, and Movies

Slides, photographs, and videotapes of stages in the Center's development, special events, students at work, the actual work of each student, innovative procedures, interesting exhibits, and openings of shows can be used for publicity, documentation, and in applying for grants.

Slides and photographs are used in the reproduction of color and black and white pictures in newspapers and magazines, on posters, on postcards, and in books. They represent a rich source for research and investigation by interns, art historians, critics, teachers.

Slides and photographs are useful as a permanent record in the event art works are destroyed, lost, or stolen.

For the above reasons, slides and photographs should be of the best professional quality and should be stored in a safe and convenient way. It may be important to consider having a duplicate set of slides and photographic negatives stored separately for safekeeping.

Very interesting and instructive slide shows can be prepared and sent to groups throughout the U.S. and other countries. The slides are the raw material.

Videotapes and movies are excellent methods for recording important happenings in the Art Center. With proper editing they can be used on television shows, in movie theaters and on cable channels. They can be shown to interested corporations and foundations, and can be used for fund-raising purposes.

Another excellent use of videotapes and movies is for teaching purposes. The artist-students of the Center gain much from seeing themselves, their interaction with others, and from seeing their work. Teachers become aware of many aspects including the art work, the methods of teaching, the environment, and the behavior of the students.

People taking classes can gain much from studying these videotapes and films.

20 Creative Art Classes in an Existing Organization

Although this book has been concerned chiefly with setting up and conducting an independent Art Center for adults with disabilities, we believe that many organizations and schools serving disabled children and adults have much to gain by including creative art classes as an integral component of their program. Much of what we have written in this book is applicable with modifications to setting up art classes within an existing organization.

Among the organizations which should include creative art classes for persons with disabilities are:

- o Schools (elementary, secondary, college)
- o Sheltered workshops
- o Community centers
- o State institutions for mentally ill and developmentally disabled
- o Recreation centers
- o Hospitals
- o Convalescent hospitals
- o Senior citizen centers
- o Board and care homes
- o Cerebral palsy programs
- o Juvenile halls
- o Prisons

Setting up art classes is relatively easy since the organization already exists, has space and students. Only additional funds for an art teacher and art supplies are required.

The most difficult task is to educate the organization's Director or Principal and the Board of Directors or School Board concerning the benefits creative art classes bring to people with disabilities. The inclusion of an imaginative art program not only benefits these persons, but can also change the organization's attitudes and expectations.

Benefits to Students

A whole new experience opens up to the student taking art classes. It is a time to let loose the imagination, to dream, to experiment without threat of failure or competitiveness, to explore a whole new world of feelings about oneself and the world we live in. The student looks around him and sees the environment with new and awakened interest.

Students receive satisfaction from being able to express their ideas and feelings through the art experience. The creating of art is a force which helps to integrate the personality.

Students' attitudes about themselves change. They develop pride and a feeling of accomplishment.

Stimulation of thinking occurs since art is not repetitive and the artist seeks new forms, new methods, new materials and learns to concentrate.

Creating art is learning through experience—learning to observe the world around us, learning to set down what we observe, learning the meaning of textures, shapes, lines, colors, black and white, learning to use materials, to use one's hands in a constructive manner.

Art is learning to cooperate with others in projects such as murals, class activities, mosaic projects.

Benefits to the Organization or School

The creative art class focuses the organization on the students' development and accomplishments. It introduces interesting, stimulating activities.

Art produced in the classes can be exhibited both within the organization and in the community, thereby improving the organization's public image and its relations with the public.

The art class brings interested persons into the organization as visitors, volunteers, interns, student aides, and advocates.

The art class involves people, organizations, and businesses as contributors of money and supplies.

The Creative Art Experience

Creative art classes, whether they be in children's or adult programs, have as their goal the release of the creative energy that lies deep within each person, and the integration and growth of the total personality. Creative art leads to an experience that cannot be duplicated. This life-enriching experience should not be denied to anyone.

Classes must be regularly scheduled. The student should be free to create, usually in paint or clay. No specific subject matter should be required and no skill emphasized. The person is free to create whatever he chooses—perhaps a head, a landscape, an abstraction. He may use brilliant colors or he may use dark ones. He may paint with light thin strokes or he may paint the surface over and over again. If he uses clay, he may roll thin shapes or he may create heavy massive shapes. The person makes the media respond to his desires. For this moment, he alone is the creator, the master. The teacher is there to stimulate, to encourage, to help when needed, but not to dictate.

How Do Creative Art Classes Start?

The program may start in different ways. Either the Board and/or the Director feel the need for innovative stimulating classes in art and decide to initiate them, or a person or organization dedicated to promoting a creative art program for persons with disabilities contacts the organization and offers to help set up such art classes.

If the organization has a governing Board, it is important they understand fully the need for and expectations of the program. This can be accomplished by a question and answer period, showing of films, bringing students from other art programs to demonstrate, or by exhibiting work from other Art Centers. The Board can be invited to visit classes in progress in other places.

An example of how one Director felt the need for art classes and acted upon it is the following:

> Mr. Silvester, Director of a school for cerebral palsied children, felt that the children were not getting enough stimulation. Due to the severity of their handicaps, art was not included in the curriculum. He presented his thoughts to his Board of Directors, showing them examples of art work done in a program for handicapped adults. The Board felt it would be a decided advantage

Bulletin

CONTRA COSTA CHILDREN'S COUNCIL

Child Care Resource & Referral Newsletter   *December/January 1986-87*

New Program for Disabled Children

The Institute of Art and Disabilities is offering a stimulating opportunity in the arts for handicapped children and youth. Through painting, sculpture, and printmaking, students will experience the tremendous joy of successful accomplishment.

Art classes will be held on Saturdays at the Institute of Art and Disabilities, 233 South 41st Street, Richmond, CA 94804. A small monthly fee of $10.00 will cover the cost of art supplies. Scholar-ships are available.

The Institute of Art and Disabilities is a comprehensive art center founded on the belief that creativity is the highest level of human functioning, and that all persons, no matter how severely disabled, have the right to develop their creativity for their own growth, prevocational development, and for the enrichment of society. For information and registration, phone the Institute at 620-0290. □

if their students were exposed to this type of stimulation. After much deliberation, they authorized the hiring of a half-time art teacher for one year.

A room was cleared, shelves were built, and art materials ordered. The art teacher was a recent graduate of an art school who, as a student, had completed an internship in an Art Center for disabled adults. She was enthusiastic about working with handicapped children and had the interest and knowledge to start the program. After much trial and tribulation, the art program took off and a year later the teacher was hired on a full-time basis.

The following is another success story:

The National Institute of Art and Disabilities felt it necessary to introduce art classes into convalescent hospitals in the area. The Directors of two convalescent hospitals were approached. Both were enthusiastic, feeling the need for their patients to engage in a constructive activity.

The Institute started by sending a staff art teacher and two of its higher-functioning students with disabilities as art aides for one morning a week to each hospital. The art classes were soon sought after by the patients. After six months, each hospital increased the time of the art classes to two mornings a week. The art aides were able to conduct the classes under the supervision of the hospitals' activities directors, with some support from the Institute. The convalescent hospitals hired the art aides and paid them above the minimum wage. A large art exhibit of the patients' art was hung in the hospitals' lobby, much to the delight of the patients, the hospital staff, and the families of the participants in the art class.

Organizational Commitments

The organization must make commitments of salary, space, art supplies, and regularly scheduled sessions. The art classes must be seen as an integral part of the development of each student or patient and not merely as an additional activity. Written records should be kept for each student of artistic, personal, and social development. A portfolio of the work of each student should be maintained in sequential order. If possible, slides of each student's work would be of decided advantage. The number of art sessions per week should be varied according to the needs of the student and to the total program of the organization. It is essential to have at least two consecutive uninterrupted hours of work per week.

The Art Teacher

Once the benefits have been established and the administration has agreed to set up the art classes, an art instructor must be hired. Hiring the right person is critical. Many problems will arise during the early stages which must be dealt with. The teacher is expected to show positive results, often under adverse conditions and in a very short time.

A trial period of at least six months is essential to demonstrate the changes that occur in the students, what they can accomplish in their art work, and how it becomes a vitalizing force to the institution or school.

The qualifications of the art teacher are the same as described in Appendix C. The teacher should be a practicing artist, preferably with an MFA degree, with some experience working with people with disabilities. The art teacher must be committed to bringing out the creative potentials of all people, no matter how severe their disability.

Staff Member Teaching Art Classes

In a small organization where funds are not available for an art teacher, the art class nonetheless can be conducted. This requires a great deal of training for the staff member who is to conduct the class. He must have continuing in-service training for as long as possible. This training should consist of both theory and practice under a qualified artist-teacher. It would be best to receive this training in an Art Center for people with disabilities where the art teacher fully understands the needs of the students. If this is not possible, the teacher should receive training in a college, university, or art school.

The teacher must understand the philosophy of a creative program, the benefits of creative self-expression for all people, especially for persons who are disabled. Theory of color, design elements, the use and appropriateness of different media and materials must be understood. There should be some comprehension of the art of the past and present in all cultures. There should be understanding of disabling conditions and behavior associated with disabilities. In order to deal with physically handicapped people, practical training must be provided in adapting equipment to meet particular needs.

Part of each training course should have sessions devoted to painting, drawing, sculpture, printmaking and other processes in which the teacher feels the need for training. The greater the participation in art experiences, the better prepared the staff member will be to carry on the classes. Without this in-service training, it is doubtful whether the program will survive at any but the most superficial level.

Space

The art studio environment should be structured so it conveys comfort and an unpressured feeling to the student. It must be totally accessible, light, airy, and large enough for the students to move around freely. Walls should be designated for showing of students' work, both in the art room and in other sections of the building. In residential facilities, the art produced may be displayed in the students' rooms as well as in public areas.

Despite the fact that a stimulating environment seems essential, art classes have been set up in highly inappropriate spaces. For example, a school recently set up an art class in a windowless basement next to the furnace. The school would never have considered the space appropriate for regular classes. Despite these adverse conditions, the class survived and eventually moved to better quarters.

Floors should be easy to clean and should not be carpeted. Students should not be afraid if water, paint, or clay is spilled or dropped accidentally. This space must be committed to the art class so that the space can be set up permanently. There should be open cabinets for students to select their own supplies and locked cabinets for specialized equipment and materials.

Regularly Scheduled Sessions

A good creative art class cannot be administered on a hit-or-miss drop-in basis. The organization and the students must make a commitment. When the sessions are regularly scheduled, the students will come with ideas they want to try out. They look forward to the next meeting with pleasurable anticipation. All students within the organization should be encouraged to try the new class. If the environment is nonjudgmental and invigorating, the teacher stimulating, most students will look forward to this experience.

Art Experiences

Tempera paints are one of the easiest and most inviting materials to use. An individual technique can be developed and the color is extremely stimulating. Water color is often preferred by older persons who may have had experience with this medium. For those who like to draw, felt pens, colored pencils, charcoal, conte crayon, and pastels can be supplied at little extra cost.

Clay is an important material in any art program. A small electric kiln can easily be installed or arrangements can be made to fire the clay in another facility with a kiln.

Acrylics can be used by students who like the feel of the viscosity of heavier material. However, this is a more expensive painting material. Oil painting is not recommended except in special circumstances, since it is more difficult to use, the clean-up process is more laborious, and it poses a fire and health hazard.

A number of printmaking processes can be engaged in without a press. These include linoleum and wood blocks, monoprints, and silk screen. Etching is not recommended because acid must be used. Many adaptations of engraving can be done. It would be a decided advantage if an etching press were available, but it is not necessary.

Many inexpensive or free materials are well-suited for collage and assemblage. These include paper wrappers, colored paper, and textured paper found in supermarkets. Natural objects such as shells, seeds, and small pieces of wood are excellent. Both of these techniques need only glue to make a finished product.

The art class, once established, becomes such an important part of the organization that it very often becomes the focus of public attention. The students themselves are the best advocates and the work exhibited in the community is the best means of promoting understanding and good will.

21 Program Evaluation and Research

Program Evaluation

In this era of accountability, on-going program evaluation is a must. Those who establish an Art Center or art classes for disabled persons must evaluate progress in achieving their goals. Honest evaluation will indicate how well the goals have been met, what strengths and weaknesses exist in the program, what remedial steps must be taken, what improvements need to be made, and what new directions should be investigated. This type of continuous evaluation makes the program more responsive to those it serves. It lays the basis for community trust and long-term support and lends credibility to the organization for financial support from government and private sources.

Evaluation should be an ongoing process, with formal narrative and financial reports which comprise the organization's annual report. During the first year, it would be wise to make frequent reports, even monthly, so that there is a firm understanding on how matters are proceeding.

It is often difficult to separate the roles and responsibiilities of the Board of Directors and the Director during the formative stages of the Art Center. The Director is appointed by the Board and bears the responsibility of carrying out the policies and goals established by the Board. At the same time, the Director must demonstrate leadership and strength in moving the program forward.

During this period, there are many questions which must be asked and answered. Some are the responsibility of the Board, some of the Director, and some are the joint responsibility of Director and Board. There is no question that unless there is a close working relationship between Director and Board, the fledgling Art Center will suffer.

The following questions are formulated in terms of an Art Center, with its Director and its Board of Directors. With slight adjustment, similar questions can be asked of a newly established art class in a school or other facility such as a hospital or senior citizen center.

Questions Addressed to the Board of Directors

- o Is the Board meeting regularly at least once a month?
- o Is Board attendance good? If not, why not?
- o How well has the Board defined the goals for the Art Center?
- o How well has the Board defined its own goals?
- o To what extent has broad community support been obtained?
- o Has the Board accomplished the following:
    - o Incorporated as a tax-exempt nonprofit corporation?
    - o Adopted by-laws?
    - o Clarified space needs, located a site, acquired a space, obtained all necessary licenses and permits?
    - o Raised "seed money" (start-up funds) and laid the ground work for future financial support?

- o Prepared a budget for a three-month period? For a full year?
- o Publicized the Center?
- o Adopted the Personnel Manual (including job descriptions Director and all staff members, and grievance procedures)?
- o Made a careful search for the Director? Appointed the most qualified applicant? Evaluated the Director during the probationary period? Set up a procedure for evaluating the Director at least once a year?

Questions Addressed to the Director

Has the Director:

- o Hired top quality staff?
- o Set up space and prepared the facility for use?
- o Are the following spaces adequate: Studio space, exhibition space, storage space, food preparation and eating space, toilet facilities, office space, library space?
- o Obtained essential and specialized equipment, furniture and supplies?
- o Set up adequate record systems in the following areas: financial records, employee records, memberships and contributions, historical records, legal records, correspondence files, mailing lists, student art records (portfolio and slides), student personal records, student case reviews?
- o Established policies and procedures for admitting students?
- o Publicized the Center?
- o Obtained community support?
- o Carried on necessary fund raising?
- o Oriented and trained staff? Provided adequate supervision of staff? Set up procedures for evaluating the job performance of each staff member at least once a year?
- o How many students have been admitted to the program?
- o Have procedures been set up to evaluate each student at least once a year?
- o Do the art teachers have a well-defined philosophy of teaching?
- o Is the studio set-up adequate for the different art media?
- o Have the needed equipment and supplies been obtained?
- o Have volunteers and interns been recruited? How well are they doing?

Questions for Both the Director and the Board of Directors

- o Is the Center exploring financial support from the following sources: fees for services, grants, memberships, fund-raising events, sales of art work produced by students, direct solicitation, gifts, wills, United Way, etc.?
- o Is the Center obtaining Adult Education and Community College instructors, graduate students and interns, corporate consultation?
- o How effectively is the Center pursuing public relations efforts with regard to the following: art exhibits in the Center and in the community, radio and TV broadcasts, posters by students, publications, workshops and conferences, open houses, students illustrating projects for other organizations, press releases, exchange visits with other programs, calendars, Very Special Arts Festivals, Disabled Artists Month?

Research

The Art Center is a fertile site for research on art and disabilities. There is a vast array of topics, theoretical and applied, which can be investigated with implications for the fields of art, psychology, education, rehabilitation, social welfare, health and human services.

Research is made possible by the very nature of the Center. A well-defined stable population is available over an extended period of time. Personal, social and medical information is available. The creative work is organized and easily accessible. A slide file of student work is maintained. Records of behavior, changes, growth, and significant incidents are kept for each student.

Among the topics under investigation are:

- o   Creativity of disabled people—including mentally ill, mentally retarded, and physically disabled.
- o   Comparative studies of the creativity of artists with disabilities and artists without.
- o   Longitudinal studies of the creative development of persons with disabilities.
- o   Relationship of self-image to growth in creative expression.
- o   Relationship between social competency and creativity.
- o   Studies of all aspects of the environment which contribute to creativity.
- o   The role of the art teacher in developing creativity.
- o   Influence of the art teacher in developing "styles" among the students.
- o   The individuality of each student's approach to creative problems.
- o   The most appropriate methods of teaching creative art to people with disabilities.
- o   Development of adaptations for physically handicapped artists.
- o   The relationship between creativity and the physical health of persons with disabilities.
- o   The relationship between creativity and the mental health of persons with disabilities.
- o   The role of staff expectations in developing people with disabilities as artists.
- o   The relationship between self-portraits and self-image in persons with a disability.

The studies and research now being conducted in Art Centers for people with disabilities will lead to a more profound understanding of the part that creativity plays in the life and growth of all individuals and of society.

IV.
An Ideal Whose
Time Has Come

The National Institute of Art and Disabilities

Juliet
Holmes

22 The National Institute of Art and Disabilities

This book ends with a dream which is only the beginning. With the success of Art Centers for people with disabilities in different communities, the need for a national center becomes apparent: The National Institute of Art and Disabilities (NIAD).

The National Institute of Art and Disabilities will be able to accomplish much that local Art Centers cannot do because of lack of prestige, lack of funds for experimentation, research and training, and lack of ability to disseminate their findings nationwide.

When we set up our first Art Center 15 years ago, it also was a dream. Like all dreams, many felt it was too early, too off-beat, too innovative, too impractical to succeed. We have proved, in these years, that when a dream is sound, when it adds to the quality of life, when there is dedication, it can become an actuality and it can succeed. When it has proven itself and has become successful, others will follow.

In 1973 there was only one Art Center for people with disabilities in California. At present there are at least ten successful Centers in California, and others are springing up around the country. These are all local Art Centers established in response to local needs.

What is the difference between local Art Centers and the National Institute of Art and Disabilities? The National Institute is a comprehensive Center where new ideas are tested, where people are trained in a practical setting, where information is gathered and disseminated. Artists, art researchers, teachers, psychologists, and social service professionals come to observe, to experiment, to learn, and to bring back ideas to their communities. Information will be disseminated throughout the nation by means of workshops, conferences, exhibits, TV, radio programs, publications, computer network.

In this book we are presenting the ideal toward which we are striving. Of course, as we continue and progress in this field we will make changes. But at this writing, our vision and goal is to develop the National Institute of Art and Disabilities as a total comprehensive Art Center.

As conceptualized, the National Institute of Art and Disabilities is a whole composed of many parts, each part adding significantly and sustaining the vigor of the total ideal. Most of the programs described are functioning at the present time but some are still in their infancy. The scope must be broadened and new ideas must be made into reality.

In the following section we describe the ideal as if it were already in complete functioning order, with the understanding that all of these components will be functioning in the very near future.

COMPONENTS OF THE INSTITUTE

The Creative Art Studio

The Creative Art Studio is the heart of the Institute. Creativity is the highest functioning of the human being. The studio is the living proof that creativity is not limited to the few but exists in all people, no matter how disabled.

Creative Art Program for Adults. Artist-students work at their own pace, without pressure, and create original paintings, sculptures, prints, and crafts of high artistic quality. They work in a well-equipped, fully accessible studio under the stimulation of master artist-teachers. They make field trips to places of artistic interest such as museums, galleries, and artists' studios. If possible, they attend five days a week, six hours a day. They are working artists and regard themselves as such, and are regarded as artists by the community.

Their art is exhibited in the Institute's gallery and in a wide variety of places, including outside galleries, public buildings, churches, corporate headquarters, banks, museums. They enter juried and nonjuried shows. When their work is sold, they receive an artist's share of the receipts.

Pre-Vocational Training. For some disabled artist-students, the creative art program can also be a pre-vocational program. Before being prepared for any kind of work, they must develop a positive self-image. They must learn to get along with their peers and their teachers. Good work habits, punctuality and good attendance, independence, courtesy, and regard for others must be inculcated. Taking care of their own needs, such as proper dress and care of equipment, is also an important part of learning good citizenship. They must learn to respect their art and the art of others.

Vocational Training. Students with disabilities who have proved themselves are trained to become *paid* Art Aides in convalescent hospitals, children's art programs, preschools, etc. They are trained in the creative art studio of the Institute for six months before they work in the community under the supervision of an Institute art teacher. Their training consists of the above-described fine art training and pre-vocational training as well as intensive training as an Art Aide. The art teacher trains them in the community facility until they are ready to work under the supervision of the staff of the facility where they will be employed. Art Aides continue to work in the art studio on a part-time basis.

Students trained in the art studio are also trained to work on the art press. They work as designers and printers of art for outside agencies and businesses under the close supervision of the master print teacher. They learn the different processes of art printing and must become proficient in the care of the press and in cleanup. If their work is sold, they share in the receipts. Those who are capable will be trained for jobs as helpers in print shops in the community.

Creative Art Classes for Children and Adolescents. On Saturdays, children and youth, both those with disabilities and those without, work in various media in the studio. They also go on trips to museums. This is a much less intensive program than the one for adults. Children go to school during the week and the art work on Saturdays becomes an enrichment program. One of the primary goals is to develop this program so that art will become a major interest in their adult lives. Another goal of this program is to encourage the schools to incorporate art into their curriculum once they have seen the value of the work of the Institute's Saturday program.

Training of Professionals

One of the most important roles of the Institute is to train professionals to become proficient in this field as administrators, teachers, and researchers. The studio provides a receptive environment for professionals to test the practicality of teaching methods, innovative ideas on creativity, on art teaching, on behavioral changes, and on the growth of individuals. People never before involved in this field are encouraged to enter this emerging profession.

The Institute awards a Certificate as a Specialist in Art and Disabilities upon completion of designated course work at the Institute and an internship. The course work is both theoretical and practical, taught by specialists in the field. The internship takes place at the Institute and in other Art Centers or classes for people with disabilities approved by the Institute.

Credit is available for in-service training and continuing education in a variety of professions such as education, nursing, psychology, medicine, social work, etc.

Conferences, seminars, workshops, and lectures are offered for professionals and the general public. Faculty is available to provide these services wherever needed.

Gallery, Exhibits, Sales, Rentals

A professional Art Gallery is an integral part of the Institute. Here artist-students display their work as artists. There are group shows, one-person shows, one-medium shows, etc. Here, artists, both disabled and nondisabled, who already have achieved a reputation exhibit their art together with the artist-students of the Institute.

Since the artist-students are working as professional artists in an art studio, their work is prepared for exhibition and sale or rental in a professional manner.

Not only is their art exhibited in the Gallery but also in other appropriate settings whenever possible. They enter both juried and nonjuried shows. They compete for commissions and for awards.

Money from the sale of art work goes to the individual artist. A small commission is retained by the Institute. This adds much to their perception of themselves as productive working artists. It also has great influence on their families, relatives, friends, and the general public.

Much recognition for the Institute comes as the result of the high artistic merit of the work and its astonishing expressiveness. David Z. Lerner wrote in the *East Bay Express*, October 31, 1986, after accidentally coming upon an exhibit by the artist-students of the National Institute of Art and Disabilities:

> But this work was powerful. Much of it gave off the kind of heat not often found emanating from community art shows—brilliant colors clashing strangely, but somehow in tune with each other, active brushwork that was passionate rather than self-consciously flamboyant. Even the more conventionally styled representational work had a certain blunt force.

Permanent Collection. A Permanent Collection of distinguished art work by the artist-students and photographs of the artists by outstanding photographers will be maintained by the Art Gallery. These will be shown in the Art Gallery, or loaned for specific exhibits, but will remain the property of the Institute.

Marketing

The public acknowledges the excellence of the art produced by the Institute's artist-students. Aware of this precious commodity, the Institute employs a skilled Marketing Specialist to find new and innovative ways to sell the work.

Paintings, sculpture, and prints are sold to corporations, banks, hotels, hospitals, government agencies, private individuals.

Art work suitable for cards, announcements, book marks, and posters can be sold as originals or reproduced for commercial production.

The exciting works in brilliant color and unusual design are easily transferred to textiles, knapsacks, T-shirts, and paper goods such as napkins, tablecloths, and shopping bags.

It is essential that an experienced, imaginative, and innovative Marketing Specialist be employed to explore these and many other possibilities.

The benefits are far-reaching. The students benefit from the growth of their self-esteem and the monetary returns from their art. The public develops an improved image of people with disabilities as productive citizens, and is enriched by their art. The Institute is justified in its philosophy that "All people are creative, regardless of disability."

A gift shop on the premises sells the art produced in the Studio.

Library

The library makes available relevant books, magazines, articles, slides, films, tapes, videotapes, and picture files. These are classified for easy accessibility.

One of the most important components of the library is a collection of slides of artist-student work. Each artist-student is represented, with slides showing the development in their art. These slides will provide endless study and inspiration for professional students of the Institute. They will provide unending material for lectures and presentations about the creativity of disabled people and the goals of the Institute.

The library also includes videotapes and films on the Institute both for inspiration and teaching.

Books, Slides, Films, Videotapes, Picture Collections

For Teachers and Professionals
- o   Work of artist-students of the Institute
- o   Art of all ages
- o   Primitive art
- o   Outsider art
- o   Folk art
- o   Art of mentally ill and mentally retarded people
- o   Unconventional and controversial art
- o   Art Brut
- o   Naive art

Teaching
- o   Books and articles published by the Institute
- o   Growth and development
- o   Theory and practice of art teaching
- o   Educational psychology
- o   Art teaching of people with disabilities
- o   Adaptations for disabled persons to enable them to engage in art

Disabilities
- o   Mentally ill
- o   Mentally retarded
- o   Physical disabilities
- o   Rehabilitation

For Artist-Students
- o Art books
- o Picture books of high quality
- o Art magazines
- o Magazines with excellent pictures, e.g., *National Geographic*
- o Picture files and slides showing the art of all ages and all civilizations
- o Picture files and slides showing flowers, animals, buildings
- o Artistic photography books showing all aspects of the world we live in
- o Imaginative, surrealistic, and expressive films and videotapes
- o Films of interesting art events

For Public Relations
- o Photographs of the art work of Institute artist-students
- o Photographs of the students at work
- o Special events of the Institute
- o Articles about the Institute published in books, magazines, and newspapers
- o Reproductions of art work by Institute students for outside agencies

Publications

Built into the Institute is the technical capability of producing publications, films, photographs, videotapes, and slides. These are aimed at different audiences, among them artists, professionals in the field of art and disabilities, psychologists, social workers, teachers, disabled artists, art students, and the general public.

Books, Pamphlets, and Monographs. In these times of advanced computer technology the task of publishing has been made much simpler. The Institute publishes books, pamphlets, and monographs. These are both of a technical nature for professionals and popular works for the general public.

Art books will be published for those who have serious reading disabilities. Most art books for this population are childish, with emphasis on copying and on leisure craft activities. The Institute publishes training manuals on methods of working creatively in paints, clay, wood, fiber, found objects, with many illustrations of significant work accomplished by disabled artist-students and by other artists.

Other publications include newsletters, articles, calendars, brochures, colored reproductions, postcards of artist-students' work, announcements, and catalogs of Institute shows.

Videotapes and Films. Films and videotapes are excellent for teaching, for publicity, and for keeping permanent records. Their great advantage is the dynamic movement and sound they record. Seeing a still photograph or a slide of a person painting can never capture the expressiveness of the movement of the body and the changes in the facial expression, nor can the photograph or slide capture the person's ability to make choices. The film or videotape can show the artist's process of finding two objects that belong together, the right two colors that belong together, or two shapes that belong together.

Slides. Slides are inexpensive, easy to duplicate, and are an excellent way of recording and showing visual images. They can be made into photographs for reproduction purposes. They can be made by amateurs (though professional slides are preferred) to show daily changes, thus keeping a running record of the studio, of the students and their artwork, and of special events.

They can be arranged and rearranged to bring out specific ideas and can be easily shown to groups and individuals. They form an excellent source for study, for teaching, for advocacy, for public awareness of the Institute, and for fund raising.

Slides are essential for keeping records of each student's art work, and of the work exhibited and sold. They are often needed to enter the art of the students into juried shows, and are often used to sell the work.

Photographs. The Institute photographs its artist-students, their methods of working, and their art work. Photographs are also made of special events, visitors to the Institute, and visits to other places of interest—other Art Centers, artists' studios, etc.

Photographs when taken with sensitivity can be an inspirational force, especially when reproduced in newspapers and newsletters.

Photographic essays are an essential part of many exhibitions and without words tell the story of the Institute and its artist-students.

Public Education and Advocacy

Every attempt is made to reach the general public through exhibits, lectures, media presentations, and publications. Many different aspects are emphasized, such as "Abilities of People with Down's Syndrome," "Importance of Adaptations in Enabling Disabled Persons to be Creative in the Arts," "Communication Through the Arts for Those Who Cannot Speak," "Art as a Preventative Against Deterioration."

The Institute's staff engages in advocacy by presentations to legislators, parents, the general public, service clubs.

Conferences, seminars, lectures, and exhibitions are held for professionals and the general public in which the latest research and methods are discussed and shown through videotapes, slides and movies.

Articles by art critics, reporters, and staff members are published in newspapers and magazines with illustrations.

Networking—Information and Referral

The Institute serves as an information and referral source. People will be able to use computers, to write or telephone for information concerning all aspects of art and disabilities. Updated files are kept on disabled artists, conferences, Art Centers, university and college art classes, publications, exhibitions. This information is stored in a computer for easy retrieval.

Every effort is made to promote networking, to improve communication, to prevent duplication of services, and to support those interested in the creativity of people with disabilities.

Consultation and Program Development

The Institute staff consults with schools, individuals, and groups in establishing and operating Art Centers and art classes for people with disabilities and in developing art programs for children and adults in schools, sheltered workshops, convalescent hospitals, and state institutions.

The Institute invites people from the United States and other countries to spend time at the Institute becoming familiar with its program and techniques. As the popularity of Art Centers increases, more communities will wish to establish Art Centers or gain more knowledge in carrying on already established Art Centers. The Institute will have files, books, slides, films, photographs, tapes, a computer, and other resources which will help administrators, teachers, and others interested in the field.

In order to help Art Centers and art classes for disabled persons to evaluate their progress in achieving their goals, the Institute is available for consultation on program development and evaluation.

Research

The Institute conducts research and disseminates the findings on many aspects of art and disabilities. It undertakes studies in areas which have been neglected, although of profound significance. Collaboration with other groups interested in these areas is welcomed. Students taking courses in the Institute are encouraged to work on these projects:

o   Longitudinal studies of creative development in the arts
o   Relationship between creative self-expression in the arts and personal and social adjustment
o   Adaptations to enable physically handicapped persons to engage in creative activities
o   Creativity of persons with Down's Syndrome
o   Videotape studies of changes in behavior correlated with advancement in art
o   Latest and experimental methods of teaching art to people with disabilities
o   Breaking down of stereotypes through art
o   Individual disabled artists
o   Compilation of group of disabled artists - pictures and biographies
o   History and work of the National Institute of Art and Disabilities
o   Approaches to the same subject matter by different disabled artist-students
o   Art experiences for disabled people

Every attempt will be made to publish this research in professional journals, in monographs, and in books. Popularized versions of the research will be published in newspaper articles, magazines, and pamphlets, and will be presented on television and radio broadcasts.

Conclusion

We believe that the establishment of a comprehensive National Institute of Art and Disabilities will not only greatly increase the number of Art Centers for disabled people throughout the United States but will also encourage many organizations to establish art programs and art classes in their communities. Training will greatly increase the number of people with expertise in this field. Some who have never considered art and disabilities as a vocation will find rewarding careers as artists, teachers, or administrators.

The Institute will work to change stereotypes that for so long have hampered disabled people from fulfilling their potentials in the art field. The studies and research conducted by the Institute will lead to more profound understanding of the part creativity plays in the life and growth of all people and of society—for truly "WE ARE ALL ONE."

CARMELO GANNELLO   Seeing Hand   Linoleum Print

I am thankful to God that I have sufficient vision to see the things around me, and that I am able to put my feelings on canvas to portray what I feel deep within my soul. My art is made up, not only of seeing, but is in three parts, searching, feeling, and spiritual portrayal of the very essence of life. I am keenly aware of life, and view it every day with fresh receptive ideas. Art must always go on and advance to new eras to keep it vibrantly alive.

I would have to say my disability has greatly influenced my art. It has definitely changed from largely representational to a semi-abstract style. I use the black circles and blobs which are illuminated by lightning bright flashes which I see constantly in my vision as an art form in my work, and I must say, my handicap has changed my life and work, I think, for the better.

CARMELO GANNELLO - SEEING HAND

Adaptations for People with Disabilities

Many people who have the desire to do art work, painting, sculpture, printmaking, or creative crafts have been denied this tremendous opportunity for expression and growth because they have not been able to handle the materials. With proper adaptations almost all of these persons are able to work. It almost seems as if there has been a conspiracy of doing nothing—both psychologically as well as physically—to bring this form of self-actualization within the range of their abilities.

For those who are mentally retarded or emotionally disabled, all that is required is modifying the environment to adapt to their needs. A permissive studio, unpressured and unhurried, supportive and noncompetitive, is essential. Under the proper conditions, these persons can blossom into outstanding artists fulfilling both their personal needs and enriching the lives of all of us.

For those who are physically disabled, specialized equipment must be developed. Each person must be studied individually. One solution will not work for all people. *In our experience we have never found anyone who has some use of hands, fingers, feet, or head who cannot engage in art work.*

Simple homemade devices have worked well. Expensive, elaborate commercially manufactured adaptation devices are not always good nor do they necessarily answer the needs of a particular handicapped artist.

PAINTING AND DRAWING

Painting with tempera is the simplest and most direct medium for painting, especially for those with physical disabilities. A few simple suggestions can help a teacher set up a painting program.

If a student has been knocking paint jars over, a wooden box with individual holes to hold each jar of paint can be constructed. The whole box can easily be clamped to the table to avoid knocking it over.

If the person is so lacking in motor control that he cannot place the brush in the jar, the paints can be put directly into muffin tins and the tins clamped to a table or board. Since a different brush cannot be placed in each cup of the muffin tin because of its shallowness, clean water will have to be provided to wash the brush. Water can be placed in one- or two-pound coffee cans. Stones should be placed in the cans to weight them down so they will not be knocked over.

It may be asked why muffin tins are not used for all people. First, there is no way of closing them to preserve the paints overnight or longer. Second, colors get muddy easily owing to their close proximity and it is impossible to clean or replace one color alone, resulting in great waste of paints since the whole tray must be emptied and refilled. Third, this arrangement does not give students flexibility in choosing or mixing their own colors. Muffin tins with paints poured directly in them should be used only as a last resort.

Brushes, which are so important, may need special modifications to make it possible for students to grasp them comfortably with their fingers, hands, toes, mouth, or head. Once a

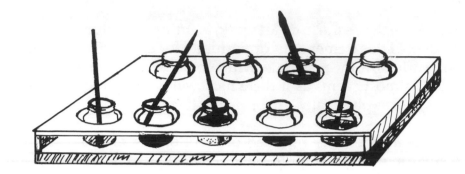

Make holes in 1/4" plywood large enough to hold baby food jars

Make base same size from heavy wood about 1" thick

Make 2 sides about 1-3/4" (high enough to hold jars but not to obstruct view of paint in jars

Glue and nail as shown

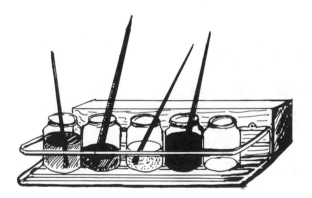

Commercial spice rack nailed to a 2" x 4" to add weight and to prevent movement

© F. LUDINS-KATZ 1983

RACKS TO HOLD PAINT JARS FROM SLIPPING

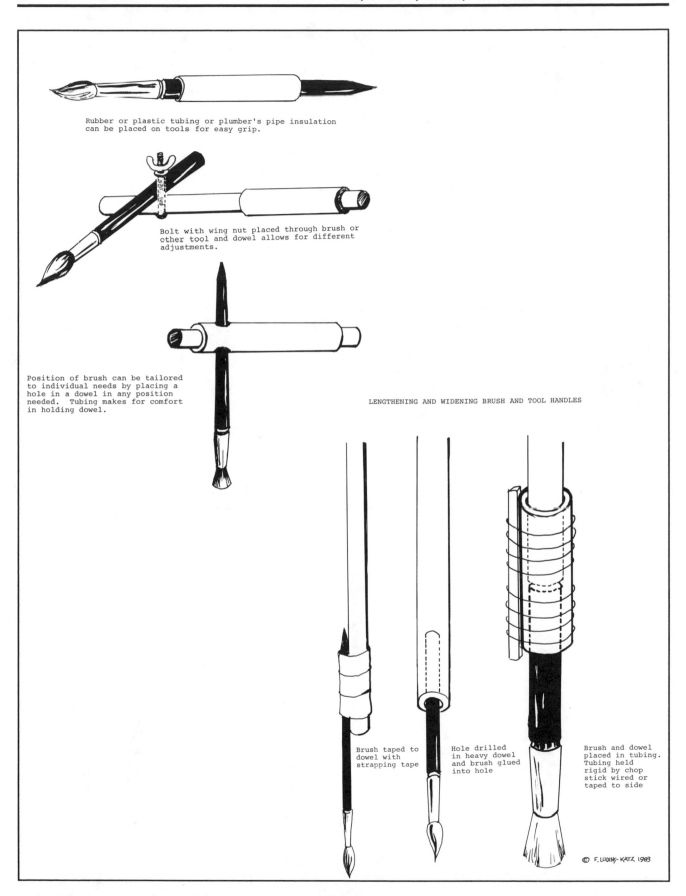

Rubber or plastic tubing or plumber's pipe insulation can be placed on tools for easy grip.

Bolt with wing nut placed through brush or other tool and dowel allows for different adjustments.

Position of brush can be tailored to individual needs by placing a hole in a dowel in any position needed. Tubing makes for comfort in holding dowel.

LENGTHENING AND WIDENING BRUSH AND TOOL HANDLES

Brush taped to dowel with strapping tape

Hole drilled in heavy dowel and brush glued into hole

Brush and dowel placed in tubing. Tubing held rigid by chop stick wired or taped to side

© F. LUDINS-KATZ 1983

ADAPTATIONS OF BRUSHES AND OTHER TOOLS

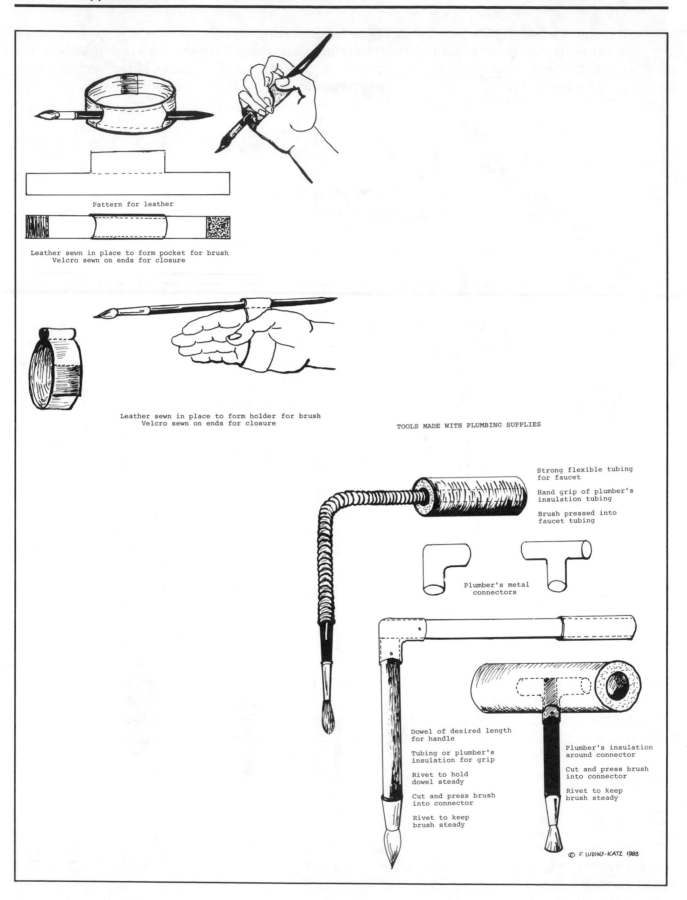

Pattern for leather

Leather sewn in place to form pocket for brush
Velcro sewn on ends for closure

Leather sewn in place to form holder for brush
Velcro sewn on ends for closure

TOOLS MADE WITH PLUMBING SUPPLIES

Strong flexible tubing
for faucet

Hand grip of plumber's
insulation tubing

Brush pressed into
faucet tubing

Plumber's metal
connectors

Dowel of desired length
for handle

Tubing or plumber's
insulation for grip

Rivet to hold
dowel steady

Cut and press brush
into connector

Rivet to keep
brush steady

Plumber's insulation
around connector

Cut and press brush
into connector

Rivet to keep
brush steady

© F. LUDINS-KATZ 1983

AIDS FOR HOLDING BRUSHES, CLAY TOOLS, FELT PENS, ETC.

person can use a brush many of the problems of painting vanish.

In drawing, the problem is holding drawing materials—pencils, chalk, pastel, charcoal, conte crayon, lithographic crayon, etc.—which may be too small to grasp. However, adaptors can easily be made for these. Many of the suggestions for adapting brushes can be used for adapting drawing materials. This would make it possible for those who enjoy the drawing process to engage in it.

Painting for Blind Persons

Most legally blind persons have some residual sight and could use the same paints used by others. However, when people's vision is so poor or when they are totally blind, paints must be specially adapted for their use.

Finger painting would be the simplest way to paint. Different textures could be improvised. Touch becomes more important when sight does not exist.

Tempera paint could be mixed with different materials such as cornstarch and soap for smoothness, starch to make the paint globby, different grades of sand from very fine to very coarse, sawdust. Each textured paint is placed in one of the compartments of a muffin tin, giving the artist a number of textures to choose from.

It would be best for the blind person to make the decision as to whether each texture should be in a different color paint or that all textures should be mixed with one color. Another method would make the textures correspond to the different values or intensities of the color—the deeper the value or the more intense the color, the rougher the texture. This type of discussion and decision-making gives the blind person control of what his painting means to him.

Tables and Easels

With very little carpentry skill one can make special tables and easels for those who could not work without their special needs being considered. Few centers can afford a professional carpenter. Of course a Center can be lucky enough to have a volunteer or a high school or college woodworking class willing to help. It is of greater importance that these constructions be sturdy and adapted for special needs than that they be elegant. Of course a professional carpenter can do both and the results would be a pleasure to look at as well as being practical.

An example of construction for an individual can be cited. The Institute admitted a young lady without arms and with only one stump with toes. She had considerable dexterity with her toes. She could hold a pencil and write. However, she could not reach the floor from her wheelchair nor could she raise her stump high enough to reach the table. After careful evaluation and consultation with her, the Institute constructed a sturdy table of just the height that was comfortable and enabled her to get many hours of joy painting and drawing.

SCULPTURE

Clay Sculpture

Clay sculpture needs very few adaptations. Work is done directly with the fingers, hands, or toes. Digging into soft clay poses few problems. If hands or feet cannot be used, tools can be held in the mouth. Sculpting tools can be modified in the same way as brushes so that physically disabled people will be able to use them.

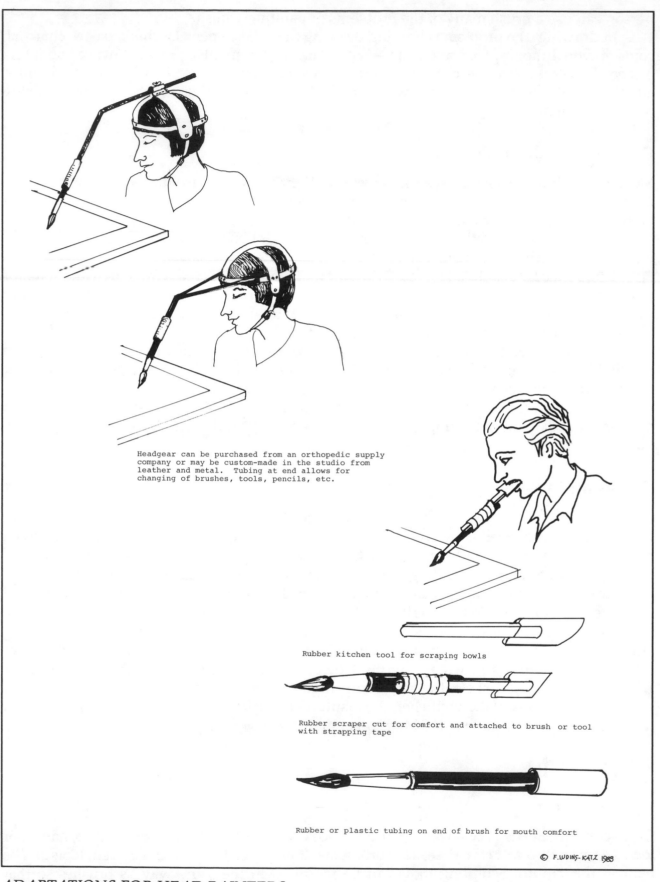

Headgear can be purchased from an orthopedic supply
company or may be custom-made in the studio from
leather and metal. Tubing at end allows for
changing of brushes, tools, pencils, etc.

Rubber kitchen tool for scraping bowls

Rubber scraper cut for comfort and attached to brush or tool
with strapping tape

Rubber or plastic tubing on end of brush for mouth comfort

© F.LUDINS-KATZ 1983

ADAPTATIONS FOR HEAD PAINTERS

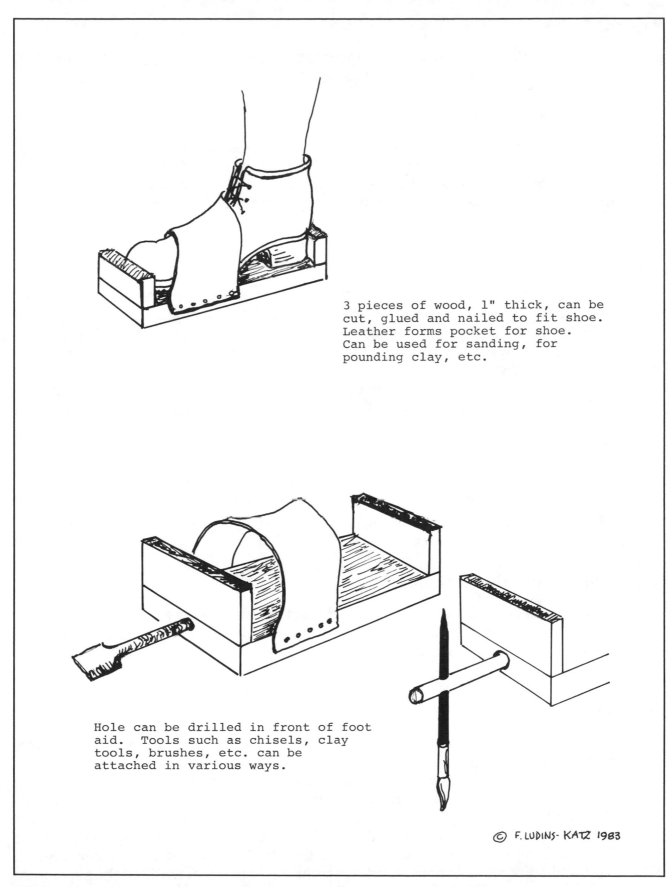

3 pieces of wood, 1" thick, can be cut, glued and nailed to fit shoe. Leather forms pocket for shoe. Can be used for sanding, for pounding clay, etc.

Hole can be drilled in front of foot aid. Tools such as chisels, clay tools, brushes, etc. can be attached in various ways.

© F. LUDINS-KATZ 1983

FOOT AID MADE FROM LEATHER AND WOOD

Papier Mache

Everything that applies to clay sculpture applies to papier mache. It would be much easier to work with paper pulp than strips of paper for most physically disabled people.

Wood and Stone Sculpture

Wood and stone sculpture is much more difficult since most severely physically disabled persons do not have the strength and control for carving these materials. Unless there is a helper who can work directly with the disabled person and follow his directions, it is best to avoid this form of art. If the person is insistent and funds are available, a helper can serve as the hands of the disabled artist.

Sculpture for Blind Persons

All types of sculpture are available. Clay and papier mache pose no problem of any kind. In fact, a blind person may be even more sensitive to the touch of the material.

In wood and stone sculpture most blind people are capable of using all the sculptor's tools. If, however, some are fearful of chisels, soft wood and soft stone, which require only files and sandpaper, can be substituted.

Working with found objects poses no difficulty. Most blind persons are very sensitive to different shapes and textures and can easily put them together with glue, cord, or nails.

PRINTMAKING

Each different process of printmaking must be carefully examined by the teacher and the student in joint communication. Together they may decide not to attempt some of the processes, but may find the majority easily made possible by using some modifications and inventions. In fact, they may even discover a new print process!

Relief Blocks and Collagraphs

People with physical disabilities very often find it easy to create relief and collagraph prints. They can push and shove shapes into position on the plate. They may require help in gluing them into place. Printing may require help but the imagination of the human being knows no bounds.

Monoprints

We had the good fortune of watching a print process being born during a workshop we were conducting. A young man with severe cerebral palsy was painting while sitting in his wheelchair. We took him out of his wheelchair and he was much more comfortable painting on the floor. Much paint was spattered around him. Someone went to get a mop. He held up his hand to stop him and motioned for us to get him a large piece of paper instead. He directed us to place the paper over the paint on the floor and began making a monoprint, using the floor as his plate. Suddenly he had an idea. He grabbed the wheelchair and ran the wheels over the paper in different directions. What a wondrous print was born when we lifted the paper from the floor amid the shouts of all participants!

Wood Blocks and Linoleum Blocks

It is very often possible for disabled people to work in wood and linoleum. For some, modifications must be made. Sometimes just having soft enough wood makes it possible for a person to carve. Using a clamp so the block stays rigid is another helpful hint. Also, placing the block on a board with wooden strips around the block stabilizes it so that it does not move and makes it possible to cut out the design no matter how shaky the hand.

For some people who cannot use their hands, a special adaptation can be made for shoes. A person with a physical disability may need help with inking and printing the block.

Engraving

Once a person can use a tool strapped to his hand, held in his mouth or toes, or attached to his head or shoe, he can create an engraving. The greatest difficulty is in inking and wiping the block, for which help may be needed.

Printing with a Press

The printing press makes possible the great joy of printing for many persons with severe disabilities. Almost all people can turn the wheel with some part of their body and watch the printed block or plate emerge as the bed of the press moves. When the paper is separated and the print is seen on the paper, the process is finished and the results are worth the effort.

Printing for Blind People

Blind persons will find planographic processes such as lithography and monoprints difficult techniques. In these processes, there are no raised or lowered surfaces and a person without vision cannot feel any difference as he works on the block or plate.

In making linoleum blocks, wood blocks, collagraphs, engravings, and other intaglio or relief processes a blind artist can easily feel his work as it progresses. These types of prints are particularly suited for people with this disability.

CRAFTS

Crafts can easily be accomplished by disabled people. Both student and teacher must make the decision which crafts to attempt and how to modify existing methods to meet the student's needs.

MATERIALS AND TOOLS FOR MAKING ADAPTATIONS FOR PEOPLE WITH PHYSICAL DISABILITIES (PARTIAL LIST)

Plumbing Supplies (for adapting brushes and drawing materials)
    Copper connectors
    Copper tubing - 1/2", 3/4", 1"
    Flexible pipe for faucets
    Pipe insulation - 1/2" to 1 1/2"
    Metal foil - copper or brass

Lumber Supplies (for making easels, tables, and boxes to hold paint jars)
    Plywood - 1/2", 3/4", 1"
    2" x 4" studs
    Assorted pieces of wood

Hardware (for adapting tools and equipment)
    Rubber and plastic tubing - 1/2", 3/4", 1", 1 1/4"
    Wing nuts
    Screws
    Rivets
    Rubber spatulas with handles (for mouth painting)
    Binding wire
    Nails

Tools
    Soldering gun and solder
    Leather punch for holes
    Wood saw
    Coping saw
    Hack saw
    Assorted drill bits up to 1" in diameter
    Hammers
    Rulers and squares
    Discarded dentists' tools
    Utility knives
    Clamps
    Drill—electric if possible
    Saws, both hand and electric

Miscellaneous
    2" and 1 1/2" velcro (or assorted widths)
    Glue for velcro
    Leather scrap
    Heavy leather needles
    Waxed thread for leather
    Chopsticks
    Sponge
    Lazy Susans

Appendix B

Free and Discounted Art Materials, Supplies, and Inappropriate Supplies

Materials used in the Art Center are often available free or at discounted prices. In obtaining free and discounted materials a certain bonus is added. It is a wonderful way to make friends and create interest in the Center. Many businesses and individuals begin to call the Center when they have materials to donate and will visit to see in what ways they can help. There is a commitment that comes with giving.

Garage sales and flea markets will often give art supplies at little or no cost once they realize the nature of the Art Center's operation. Contributors should always be told that their gift is tax deductible, and a statement of its value should be prepared for the donor.

It is advisable to make connections with wholesale and retail distributors of art supplies. Other contacts that should be made are with commercial companies that either use or distribute materials that can be used in any of the art processes. Donors of material should always be acknowledged with a thank-you note and a statement of the value of the donation for tax exemption purposes.

In some cities, there are surplus property depots and centers where art supplies donated by corporations and individuals can be obtained at little or no cost by nonprofit organizations. Such depots should be checked on a regular basis.

Paper

Paper which is so abundantly used can usually be obtained at no cost. Paper distributors, both wholesale and retail, often have stacks of paper with slightly damaged edges, paper that does not meet color standards, or papers of odd sizes. Printers purchase paper for particular jobs and often have stacks of leftovers. Errors are made in printing and sometimes the Center can procure excellent quality paper printed on one side. Printers cut paper to specific sizes for their jobs and often discard the paper they have cut off.

Really large paper printed on one side can be obtained from billboard companies since they always print more than is needed. End rolls of newsprint which cannot be used on presses, excellent for chalk and charcoal drawings, will usually be donated by newspapers.

Paper for particular jobs, such as for a book, a calendar, or posters, must often be purchased. Paper companies who know the Center will often be willing to quote a good price or make a donation.

Paint

Paint must usually be purchased. Since paints are used in large quantities they should be purchased in bulk at wholesale prices. The quality must be good enough to produce good results. Poor paint with a lot of filler that lacks vibrant color should never be bought because of its low price. It leads to poor work and frustration. Old and dried paint is another poor investment. However, the price of paint is not always a good criterion of its quality. It is therefore advisable to try a few jars of paint from different companies or a few water color boxes before a sizeable purchase is made.

In some rare instances it is possible to find paint which has been mixed incorrectly to specifications. The Center may be the beneficiary.

Brushes

Brushes last a long time and should be of good quality but need not be specialized for artists' use nor need they be expensive. Very often lacquer brushes, housepainters' brushes, and glue brushes can be used with excellent results. A great variety of brushes should be purchased—long haired, short haired, thick, thin, wide, narrow, small, large, stiff and soft haired. It is important to test brushes before purchasing in quantity. Make sure the ferrules are attached securely to the wood and the hair does not fall out or go limp when wet. All brushes should be tested before purchase.

Sometimes it is possible to purchase discontinued brushes or brushes from companies no longer manufacturing them. If you can find such companies, brushes can be bought at great savings.

Clay

In some areas clay can be dug from the earth. This is a wonderful experience for the students and the staff. Where this is not possible, a good all-purpose clay should be purchased in bulk at wholesale prices. Very often clay that has dried is contributed and can be reclaimed. Clay should never be wasted and all clay, if not fired, should be recycled.

Clay Tools

Clay tools are beautiful to look at and a joy to use. However, they are expensive. Most clay tools can be easily made in the Center. They may not look or feel as nice, but they are practical and work well. Many household implements make excellent clay tools.

Matboard

Small mat boards can be obtained free from picture frame shops since they always have much scrap left over from their framing operations. Large mat boards will have to be purchased unless framers, art supply stores, and paper suppliers donate their imperfect stock (ragged edges, off color, slightly faded or soiled).

Corrugated Cardboard

Cardboard for large portfolios and murals can be obtained free from refrigerator, mattress, appliance, and furniture stores. The packing crates from which they come are clean and large and the quality of the board is excellent. Corrugated boxes in which paper is packed can be obtained free from printing shops.

Wood

Wood scrap can be obtained free from lumber yards, cabinet shops, builders, and picture framers. Especially interesting shapes can be obtained free from pattern makers. For special projects, it may be necessary to purchase the proper wood.

Tiles

Tiles can usually be obtained free. Builders and tile contractors always buy more than is needed. Also many stores have discontinued lots and cannot sell the tile if they do not have a sufficient number of boxes on hand. Then too, tile very often is slightly off color and cannot be used for a particular job.

Collage and Assemblage Materials

Materials for these projects can always be obtained free. The supply is endless. There is a tremendous variety of natural material that one can acquire—grasses, seeds, pebbles, shells, feathers. Man-made material—metal scraps, nails, washers, beads, rope, pipes, screens, waterwashed glass—is also easily obtainable.

Another excellent way to get these materials is through discarded sample books of wallpaper, leather, trimming, etc.

Printmaking Materials

Some materials for different plates can be picked up free. Plastic, linoleum scrap, and wood suitable for blocks can usually be picked up at no cost. Metal plates will usually have to be bought. Tools can be homemade or adapted. However, really specialized material will have to be purchased from a print maker's shop or catalog. These include cutting tools, barens, brayers, and printing inks.

Fresh Cut Flowers

Fresh cut flowers, which are excellent subject matter for painting and drawing and do much to cheer the studio environment, can easily be obtained free from florists, botanical parks, and people's gardens.

Frames

Framing is a very important part of the presentation of the art. A good framing job lends an air of professionalism to the art work. Many frames can be obtained free from picture framers since pictures are brought in to be framed differently. Art galleries often remove frames when they sell pictures. Even museums dispose of frames no longer needed. Low cost frames are advertised in many art publications.

Inappropriate Materials and Equipment

Art supplies are often donated to the Center, but there are certain materials and equipment which should be refused or discarded immediately. These include:

o   Oil paints, lacquers, and solvents because of fire hazards, fumes, and clean-up problems.
o   Acids for etching because of hazardous fumes and skin burning problems.
o   Paperhanger's paste containing arsenic or other poisons.
o   Tempera paints or water color paints with excessive filler, resulting in poor color.
o   Felt pens with hazardous fumes.
o   Flimsy easels.
o   Brushes with limp or falling hair or which are paint-hardened.
o   Broken tools and equipment too expensive to repair.

Specialized Tools

Sharp tools and knives should be handled only by those students who can use them with care and without injury to themselves or others.

Measuring tools should be given to students who have learned to read and can use them.

Electrical tools must be used under careful supervision.

Looms that are too complicated for students to use should be set aside until students are capable of using them.

Personnel Manual & Job Descriptions

(Sample Personnel Manual)

This Personnel Manual, adopted by the Board of Directors on _____ , presents the rules and regulations governing the staff of the _____ . Changes in the Personnel Manual may be made only by action of the Board of Directors, must be in writing, and must be presented to the staff upon adoption.

Appointment

All employees will receive a letter of appointment specifying salary, duties, work hours, probationary period. The employees must be given an opportunity to read the Personnel Manual.

Part time employees will have the same rights, privileges, and obligations as full time employees.

Probationary Period

All employees have a specified probationary period.

During the probationary period the employee may be terminated with one week's notice without a written or oral explanation, and with no rights of appeal.

During the probationary period the employee may resign, given one week's notice.

Work Week; Work Day

All full time employees will work 37 1/2 hours per week, Monday thorough Friday, unless other arrangements are made between the Director and the employee. The work day is 7 1/2 hours.

Work hours of part time employees will be agreed upon by the Director and the employee.

Holiday

Ten holidays will be observed each year:

New Years Day	Labor Day
Martin Luther King Jr. Day	Columbus Day
Presidents Day	Veterans Day
Memorial Day	Thanksgiving Day
Independence Day	Christmas Day

By agreement of the Director and the staff holidays can be shifted as long as the total number of holidays remains 10.

Vacation

Full time employees are granted 10 days vacation per year during the first three years of employment.

For each subsequent year of full time employment one additional vacation day will be added per year up to a maximum of 15 vacation days per year.

No vacation time can be used until after being employed for six months.

Earned vacation time can be accumulated from year to year.

Part time employees will have the same vacation rules, prorated according to their percentage of full time employment.

Sick Leave

Full time employees are granted 10 days sick leave per year.

No sick leave can be used until after being employed for six months.

Sick leave can be accumulated from year to year to a maximum of 20 days.

Sick leave will not be reimbursed by cash payment.

Sick leave can be used only for verifiable sickness.

Compensatory Time

Compensatory time is time of one hour or more spent on official business beyond the designated work day.

Compensatory time must be authorized in writing by the Director.

Compensatory time will not be reimbursed by cash payment.

The Director can authorize time off for accumulated compensatory time.

Termination

During the probationary period an employee can be terminated with one week's notice, without written or verbal explanation, with no rights of appeal.

An employee who has satisfactorily completed the probationary period can be terminated with written explanation, two weeks' notice, and with rights of appeal.

Grievance Procedure

All grievances should be brought to the attention of the Director.

If the grievance cannot be resolved by the Director, the staff member has the right to bring the grievance to the Board of Directors.

Working Hours

The work week for all staff members is 37 1/2 hours; 7 1/2 hours per day.

Students attend 6 hours per day, 9:30 to 3:30 p.m. Lunch is from 1 to 2 p.m.

Art Teacher

Option 1: 8:30 a.m. to 5 p.m.

Lunch hour - 1 hour free, to coincide with student lunch hour

Option 2: 8:30 a.m. to 4 p.m.
   Eat lunch with students; on duty during student lunch hour

Secretary

8:30 a.m. to 4:30 or 5 p.m., depending on lunch period of 1/2 hour or 1 hour

Counselor

8:30 a.m. to 4:30 or 5 p.m., depending on lunch period of 1/2 hour or 1 hour

Breaks

Each staff member is entitled to a 15-minute break morning and afternoon.

Job Description

DIRECTOR

Appointed by and responsible to the Board of Directors. May be discharged by the Board.

Duties and Responsibilities
- Establishes and maintains program of highest quality; develops and maintains environment for this high quality program.
- Maintains good working relationship with Board, staff clients, other agencies.
- Attends meetings of the Board.
- Appoints and discharges all staff members; provides ongoing supervision, inservice training, evaluation of performance.
- Responsible for setting up the space, preparing the facility, selecting art experiences, supplies and equipment.
- Responsible for developing and maintaining all records relating to clients and agency.
- Resposible for selection criteria and admission of clients.
- Responsible for preparing annual budget for submission to and approval by the Board; responsible for keeping within this budget.
- Responsible for publicizing the Center and relating to the community.
- Responsible for fundraising in cooperation with the Board.
- Prepares annual report. Responsible for setting up and implementing long range goals in cooperation with the Board.
- Carries on other duties and responsibilities as required by the Board.

Qualifications
- Master of Fine Arts degree or equivalent.
- At least three years successful experience in setting up and/or operating art programs, or equivalent experience.
- Practical experience in teaching art to persons with disabilities.
- Practicing artist preferred.

Work Week: 35 hours

Probationary Period: 3 months, during which time may be dismissed without cause

Salary: $15,000 to $18,000 per year

Job Description

ART TEACHER

Under the direction of the Director; appointed by the Director.

Duties
- o In conjunction with all other staff, establishes and maintains a creative and pleasurable environment in the center.
- o Acts as a stimulating and inspirational force, helping each student grow to fullest capacity as a creative artist.
- o Helps establish artistic, technical, and social goals for each student, and reviews their progess in achieving these goals.
- o Maintains a portfolio of each student's work in sequential order.
- o Helps select student art work for exhibit in the studio and for outside exhibits.
- o Maintains art supplies and art equipment in orderly fashion.
- o Keeps track of and orders art supplies and equipment.
- o Helps select and prepare art materials for use by students.
- o Organizes preparation for work and for cleanup of studio.
- o Designs and uses adaptations of art supplies and equipment as needed by each student.
- o Performs other assignments as required.

Qualifications
- o MFA or equivalent; exhibiting artist preferred.
- o At least 2 years of art teaching experience, preferably with persons with disabilities.
- o Must be in tune with the Center's philosophy and student population.

Work Week: 35 hours

Probationary Period: 3 months, during which time may be dismissed without cause.

Salary: $14,000 per year

Job Description

CURATOR

Under the direction of the Director; appointed by the Director.

Duties
- o Preserves art work - sculpture, painting, prints, creative crafts.
- o With input from staff, arranges exhibitions in the Art Center's gallery.
- o With input from staff, arranges exhibits in galleries and other suitable places.
- o In charge of mounting all exhibits.
- o In charge of creating interesting shows of special interest.
- o In charge of creating announcements of exhibits.
- o In charge of arranging interesting exhibition openings.
- o Keeps track of exhibitions of each student, and of sales, including name and address of purchaser and sale price.
- o In charge of keeping up the slide collection and making slides and photographs of work.
- o (In a small Art Center, may have to do the matting and framing until the Center can afford to employ an assistant.)

Qualifications
- o MFA preferable, in Art History, museum studies, or equivalent.
- o Two years of successful experience in an art gallery, under professional supervision.
- o Must be in tune with the Center's philosophy and student population.

Work Week: 35 hours

Probationary Period: 3 months, during which time can be discharged without cause

Salary: $15,000 per year

Job Description

SOCIAL WORKER/COUNSELOR

Under the direction of the Director; appointed by the Director.

Duties

- o Relates to and communicates with social agencies, families, community care administrators.
- o Helps students work out personal or social problems which keep them from fulfilling their creative potential.
- o Identifies and recruits new students into the program.
- o Responsible for case review of all students.
- o Participates in case discussions of individual students, both in the Center and in outside agencies.
- o Maintains informational records on each student—personal, social, and medical.
- o Performs other assignments as required.

Qualifications

- o MSW. Licensed Social Worker, or Counselor.
- o Two years of experience in a social agency, preferably with persons with disabilities.

Work Week: 35 hours

Probationary Period: 3 months, during which time may be dismissed without cause.

Salary: $16,000 per year.

Job Description

MARKETING SPECIALIST

Under the direction of the Director; appointed by the Director.

Duties
- o   Locates places where the art by Institute artists can be displayed and sold.
- o   Prepares and circulates information about the art.
- o   Arranges for displays and special events in public and private buildings to bring art to prospective buyers.
- o   Sells art and obtains art commissions through wholesale and retail channels.
- o   Maintains records of contracts, art commissions, sales, exhibition sites, etc.

Qualifications
- o   In tune with the Institute's goals, methods, and art.
- o   Appreciation of the artistic quality of work by the Institute's artist-students.
- o   At least two years of successful experience in merchandising art work commercially.

Work Week: 37 1/2 hours

Probationary Period: 3 months, during which time may be dismissed without cause.

Salary: $14,000 per year

Job Description

SECRETARY

Under the direction of the Director; appointed by the Director.

Duties
- o Serves as receptionist for students and visitors.
- o Has excellent presence over the telephone.
- o Types at least 60 words per minute.
- o Maintains all records, files, and correspondence of the Center, its students and staff.
- o Keeps track of and orders all office supplies.
- o Maintains all financial records of the Center, under supervision of the Accountant.

Qualifications
- o Graduation from college or business school
- o At least two years of office management experience in community agency or business
- o Excellent typist
- o Excellent receptionist

Work Week: 35 hours

Probationary Period: 3 months, during which time may be dismissed without cause.

Salary: $12,000 per year

Job Description

ATTENDANT/AIDE

Under the direction of the Director; appointed by the Director.

Duties
- o Assists in unloading and loading buses. Helps put on and remove smocks. Prepares student for work and helps clean up student at the end of the work day.
- o Lifts and moves physically disabled students if necessary.
- o Feeds and toilets the students who need such help.
- o Prepares and distributes juices, coffee, fruit, etc. to students during breaks; cleans up after breaks.
- o If student brings lunch, helps supervise lunch period.
- o May assist the Art Teacher in straightening up shelves, in giving out and putting away supplies, etc. when not needed for the above primary needs.
- o Performs other assignments as required.

Qualifications
- o High school graduate.
- o At least one year experience working with one or more disabled persons.
- o Practical nursing training and experience preferred.
- o Must be in tune with the Center's philosophy and student population.

Work Week: 35 hours

Probationary Period: 3 months, during which time may be dismissed without cause.

Salary: $9,000 per year

Setting up the Center

(Sample)

ARTICLES OF INCORPORATION OF ART CENTER FOR DISABLED

I

The name of this corporation is ART CENTER FOR DISABLED.

II

A. This corporation is a nonprofit public benefit corporation and is not organized for the private gain of any person. It is organized under the Nonprofit Public Benefit Corporation Law for charitable purposes.

B. The specific purpose of this coporation is to provide a creative art program to persons who are mentally, physically, or socially handicapped.

III

The name and address in the State of _____ of this corporation's initial agent for service of process is:

IV

A. This corporation is organized and operated exclusively for charitable purposes within the meaning of Section 501(c)(3) of the Internal Revenue Code.

B. Notwithstanding any other provision of these articles, the corporation shall not carry on any other activities not permitted to be carried on (a) by a corporation exempt from federal income tax under Section 501(c)(3) of the Internal Revenue Code or (b) by a corporation contributions to which are deductible under Section 170(c)(2) of the Internal Revenue Code.

C. No substantial part of the activities of this corporation shall consist of carrying on propaganda, or otherwise attempting to influence legislation, and the corporation shall not participate or intervene in any political campaign (including the publishing or distributing of statements) on behalf of any candidate for public office.

V

The property of this corporation is irrevocably dedicated to charitable purposes and no part of the net income or assets of this corporation shall ever inure to the benefit of any director, officer, or member thereof or to the beneift of any private person. Upon the dissolution or winding up of the corporation, its assets remaining after payment, or provision for payment, of all debts and liabilities of this corporation shall be distributed to a nonprofit fund, foundation, or corporation which is organized and operated exclusively for charitable purposes and which has established its tax exempt status under Section 501(c)(3) of the Internal Revenue Code.

DATED: _____

_____

I hereby declare that I am the person who executed the foregoing Articles of Incorporation, which execution is my act and deed.

_____

(Sample)

BY-LAWS OF ART CENTER FOR DISABLED

Article I

The principal office of the corporation shall be located in the County of

Article II

Section 1. Membership
There shall be one (1) class of members who shall be called Friends of _____ They shall be kept informed of organizational activities, and shall have the opportunity to participate in these activities.

Section 2. Nonliability of Members
No member shall be personally liable for the debts, liabilities, or obligations of the corporation.

Section 3. Dues of Members
The dues of memberships shall be fixed annually by the Board of Directors.

Section 4. Meetings of the Membership
Meetings may be called by the President or by one-third of the Board of Directors. Written notice of the time, place and purpose of such meetings shall be mailed to members at least seven (7) days in advance.

Article III: *Directors*

Section 1. Powers of Directors
The Board of Directors shall exercise all powers conferred upon the corporation by law and shall have full power, by majority vote of the Directors present at a meeting at which a quorum is present, to adopt rules and regulations governing the action of the Board of Directors.

Section 2. Number, Election and Term of Office
At a special meeting of the Incorporators, within 90 days after adoption of these bylaws, the Incorporator shall elect a full Board of Directors, to consist of no more than 17 and no fewer than 9 Directors. The term of office shall be two (2) years. By means of a lottery at that meeting, one-half of the Directors elected shall be designated to serve a term of one year; the other half shall serve a normal term of two years. Thereafter, one-half of the Directors shall be elected each year at the annual meeting by a majority of the Directors then in office. No Director shall serve more than three (3) successive terms.

Section 4. Quorum
A quorum shall consist of one-third (1/3) of the Directors.

Section 5. Vacancies
Vacancies on the Board of Directors may be filled by vote of the remaining Directors at the annual meeting or a duly called special meeting. The Director elected to fill a vacancy shall be elected for the unexpired term of his predecessor in office.

Section 6. Regular Meetings

Regular meetings shall be at such time and place and upon such notice as the Directors may by vote provide.

Section 7. Annual Meeting

The annual meeting shall be held in the first quarter of the year at such date, time and place as may be determined by the Board of Directors.

Section 8. Special Meetings

Special meetings may be called by the President or by two Directors. Written notice of the time, place and purpose of such meetings shall be mailed to all Directors at least five (5) days in advance.

Section 9. Action without a Meeting

Any action may be taken or ratified without a meeting if every Director consents to such action in writing.

Section 10. Liabilities of Directors

Directors of this corporation shall not be personally liable for the debts, liabilities, or obligations of the corporation.

Article IV

Section 1. Number of Officers

The Directors shall elect a President, Vice-President, Secretary, and Treasurer, and such other officers as the Directors may from time to time determine. The President shall hold only one office. Remaining Directors may hold not more than two offices.

Section 2. Election and Term of Office

Those officers serving shall remain in office until the next annual meeting. Thereafter, the officers of the corporation shall also be elected at the annual meeting immediately following the election of Directors. The term of office shall be one year or until their successors are elected and qualified. Officers may be removed, with cause, by a vote of a majority of the Directors present at a meeting at which a quorum is present.

Section 3. Duties

The duties of the officers shall be as follows:

a) President - General supervision and control of the affairs of thecorporation; the President shall keep the Board of Directors fully informed and shall freely consult with them concerning the activities of the corporation; the President shall preside at all the meetings of the Board of Directors;

b) Vice-President - Perform the duties of the President when the President is not available;

c) Secretary - Keep full and complete records of the meetings and other business of the corporation; in the absence of the President and Vice-President, the Secretary shall perform the duties of the President;

d) Treasurer - Keep and maintain the books of the corporation and be responsible for the deposit of all funds of the corporation; the Treasurer shall at all reasonable times exhibit the corporate books and accounts to any officer or Director of the corporation and shall be required to prepare an annual accounting statement which must be presented to the Board at the annual meeting; in the absence of the President, Vice-President and Secretary, the Treasurer shall perform the duties of the President.

The officers shall perform such other duties as may be prescribed by the Board of Directors.

Article V: *Committees*

Section 1. *Nominating Committee*
At the annual meeting of the Directors, the Board shall elect from among the Directors a Nominating Committee of five (5) members. The Nominating Committee shall convene to select nominees for election as Directors at the next annual meeting. The Nominating Committee shall make its recommendations regarding the nominees at least 60 days prior to the ensuing annual meeting, said recommendations to be expressed in a written report sent to each Director. Said report shall contain a statement of number of Directors to be elected and a statement of qualifications of persons nominated.

Other nominations may be made by any Director by filing thereof with a statement of qualifications in writing with the Secretary of the corporation at least 15 days prior to the annual meeting.

Section 2. *Finance Committee*
The Finance Committee Chairperson shall be appointed by the President and approved by the Directors at the annual meeting. The chairperson shall appoint the other members of the Finance Committee.

Section 3. *Other Committees*
Other committees may be designated by a resolution adopted by the Directors for the period deemed necessary. Except as otherwise provided in such a resolution, chairpersons of each such committee shall be appointed by the President of the corporation and approved by the Directors. The chairpersons shall appoint other committee members. Those members may be selected from outside the Board of Directors.

Section 4. *Rules*
Each committee may adopt rules for its own government, so long as such rules are not inconsistent with these bylaws or with rules adopted by the Board of Directors.

Section 5. *Removal*
The President has the power to remove any chairperson, with cause, and with the approval of the Board.

Article VI: *Books*

There shall be kept at the office of the corporation correct books of account of the activities and transactions of the corporation, including a minute book which shall contain a copy of the Articles of Incorporation, a copy of these Bylaws, and all minutes of the meetings of the Board of Directors.

Article VII: Amendment

These bylaws may be amended or repealed by a majority vote of the Directors at a meeting called for that purpose.

(Sample)

ART CENTER FOR DISABLED APPLICATION FOR ADMISSION

The Art Center is an equal opportunity agency and does not discriminate on the basis of disability, sex, race, religion, or national origin.

Name _____ Date of Application _____
       Last   First   Middle

Address _____ Birthdate _____
      Number   Street

_____ Sex _____ Soc. Sec. No. _____
City   Zip Code

Phone _____ Referred by _____

                Agency _____

Lives with _____

Relationship to Applicant _____

Mother's Name _____ Phone (Home) _____

Mother's Address _____ Phone (Work) _____
           Street   City   Zip

Father's Name _____ Phone (Home) _____

Father's Address _____ Phone (Work) _____
           Street   City   Zip

Legal Guardian or Conservator (if any) _____

Address _____ Phone _____
      Street   City   Zip

Case Manager's Name _____ Phone _____

Case Manager's Agency _____

Other Social Agencies Involved (Include worker's name and phone):

_____

_____

Emergency Information

Date _____   Signature _____

Relationship to Student _____

Person to be contacted in case of emergency (List three names)

Name/Relationship   Address   Phone

_____

_____

_____

Name of Family Physician _____

Address _____ Phone _____
       Street   City   Zip

Medical Number _____

Current Medications Being Used:

_____

_____

Dietary Restrictions _____

_____

Chronic Medical or Physical Problems _____

_____

Describe Any Medical or Physical Problem Which Needs Attention:

_____

_____

In case of accident or serious illness, if neither parent nor emergency contacts are available, anyone who is seriously ill or injured will be taken to the nearest hospital.

PLEASE NOTIFY US IMMEDIATELY IF THERE IS ANY CHANGE IN THE ABOVE INFORMATION.

Previous History

Schools Attended:

Dates	Name of School	Address

State Institutions or Private Institutions Attended:

Dates	Name of Institution	Address

Other Programs Attended: (Include any present programs)

Dates	Name	Address	Type of Program

What are your expectations for the student's participation in the Art Center?   (Add any comments you wish.)

_____
Person Completing This Form

(Sample)

ART CENTER FOR DISABLED RELEASE FORM

The undersigned student and/or guardian give permission to the Art Center to photograph the student and/or his/her art work for publication in newspapers, magazines or any other written material, or for use on radio and television, or for exhibit.

All art work produced in the Art Center belongs to the Center, unless requested by the student and/or guardian.

If the art work is sold, a reasonable percentage of the sale price will be given to the student.

Signature of Student _____ Date _____

Signature of Guardian _____ Date _____
(if necessary)

(Sample)

ART CENTER FOR DISABLED AUTHORIZATION FOR RELEASE OF PERSONAL INFORMATION

This is to authorize release of information regarding:

Name _____ Birthdate _____

To Art Center, from:

_____
Name

_____
Address   City   Zip

From Art Center, to:

_____
Name

_____
Address   City   Zip

Information Requested: _____

_____

_____

Signed: _____ Date _____
                Student or Guardian

Witnessed by: _____ Date _____

(Sample)

ART CENTER FOR DISABLED STUDENT PROGRESS REPORT

Student Name _____ Date _____

Staff Present:

Recorder:

Review of Progress	Staff Goals	Implementation

(Sample)

RECORD OF EXHIBITS AND SALES

Name of Student: _____

Date	Exhibit/Address	Name & Address of Purchaser	Price

Client's Rights

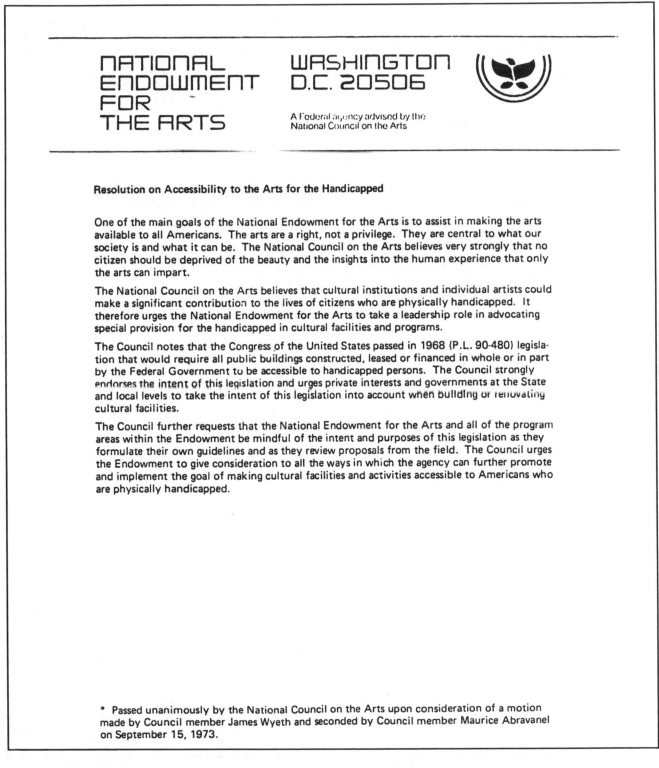

NATIONAL ENDOWMENT FOR THE ARTS

WASHINGTON D.C. 20506

A Federal agency advised by the
National Council on the Arts

Resolution on Accessibility to the Arts for the Handicapped

One of the main goals of the National Endowment for the Arts is to assist in making the arts available to all Americans. The arts are a right, not a privilege. They are central to what our society is and what it can be. The National Council on the Arts believes very strongly that no citizen should be deprived of the beauty and the insights into the human experience that only the arts can impart.

The National Council on the Arts believes that cultural institutions and individual artists could make a significant contribution to the lives of citizens who are physically handicapped. It therefore urges the National Endowment for the Arts to take a leadership role in advocating special provision for the handicapped in cultural facilities and programs.

The Council notes that the Congress of the United States passed in 1968 (P.L. 90-480) legislation that would require all public buildings constructed, leased or financed in whole or in part by the Federal Government to be accessible to handicapped persons. The Council strongly endorses the intent of this legislation and urges private interests and governments at the State and local levels to take the intent of this legislation into account when building or renovating cultural facilities.

The Council further requests that the National Endowment for the Arts and all of the program areas within the Endowment be mindful of the intent and purposes of this legislation as they formulate their own guidelines and as they review proposals from the field. The Council urges the Endowment to give consideration to all the ways in which the agency can further promote and implement the goal of making cultural facilities and activities accessible to Americans who are physically handicapped.

* Passed unanimously by the National Council on the Arts upon consideration of a motion made by Council member James Wyeth and seconded by Council member Maurice Abravanel on September 15, 1973.

NATIONAL ENDOWMENT FOR THE ARTS - STATEMENT ON ACCESSIBILITY

CLIENTS' RIGHTS -- CALIFORNIA

RIGHTS OF PERSONS WITH DEVELOPMENTAL DISABILITIES
(Welfare Institutions Code, Sections 4423, 4473, 4503 and
4504: California Administrative Code, Title 17, S.50510)

Each person with a developmental disability is entitled
to the same rights, protections, and responsibilities as all
other persons under the laws and Constitution of the State of
California, and under the laws and the Constitution of the
United States. Unless otherwise restricted by law, these
rights may be exercised at will by any person with a
developmental disability. These rights include, but are not
limited to, the following:

1. A right to treatment and habilitation services.
Treatment and habilitation services shall foster the
developmental potential of the person. Such services shall
protect the personal liberty of the individual and shall be
provided under conditions which are the least restrictive
necessary to achieve the purposes of treatment.

2. A right to dignity, privacy, and humane care.

3. A right to participate in an appropriate program of
publicly-supported education, regardless of the degree of
handicap.

4. A right to religious freedom and practice, including
the right to attend services or to refuse attendance, to
participate in worship or not to participate in worship.

5. A right to prompt and appropriate medical care and
treatment.

6. A right to social interaction and participation in
community activities.

7. A right to physical exercise and recreational
opportunities.

8. A right to be free from harm, including unnecessary
physical restraint, or isolation, excessive medication, abuse
or neglect. Medication shall not be used as punishment, for
convenience of staff, as a substitute for program, or in
quantities that interfere with the treatment program.

9. A right to be free from hazardous procedures.

10. A right to advocacy services. as provided by law, to
protect and assert the civil, legal, and service rights to
which any person with a developmental disability is entitled.

11. A right to be free from discrimination by exclusion from participation in, or denial of the benefits of, any program or activity which receives public funds solely by reason of being a person with a developmental disability.

12. A right of access to the courts for purposes including, but not limited to, the following:

a. to protect or assert any right to which any person with a developmental disability is entitled;

b. to question a treatment decision affecting such rights, once the administrative remedies provided by law, if any, have been exhausted;

c) to inquire into the terms and conditions of placement in any community care or health facility, or state hospital by way of a writ of habeas corpus, and;

d) To contest a guardianship or conservatorship, its terms, and/or the individual or entity appointed as guardian or conservator.

Each person with a developmental disability who has been admitted or committed to a state hospital, community care facility, or health facility shall have rights which include, but are not limited to, the following.

1. To keep and be allowed to spend one's own money for personal and incidental needs.

2. To keep and wear one's own clothing.

3. To keep and use one's own personal possessions, including toilet articles.

4. To have access to individual storage space for one's private use.

5. To see visitors each day.

6. To have reasonable access to telephones, both to make and receive confidential calls, and to have calls made for one upon request.

7. To mail and receive unopened correspondence and to have ready access to letter-writing materials, including sufficient postage in the form of United States postal stamps.

8. To refuse electroconvulsive therapy (ECT).

9. To refuse behavior modification techniques which cause pain or trauma.

10. To refuse psychosurgery.

11. Other rights as specified by administrative regulations of any federal, state, or local agency.

In addition, to all of the other rights provided above, each person with a developmental disability who resides in a state hospital shall be accorded the following rights:

1) If involuntarily detained, to have access to a current and up-to-date copy of the California Welfare and Institutions Code. This right includes the right to have

assistance from the Clients' Rights Advocate in the reading and understanding of Code.

2)   To give or withhold consent for treatments and procedures, in the absence of a judicial order or other provision of law which provides for the exercise of this right to devolve to another party.

3)   To be provided with the amount of funds specified in Welfare and Institutions Code Section 4473 for personal and incidental use if, following the initial thirty (30) days of state hospital residency, the person is not receiving an amount of income for such use which is equal to or greater than the amount authorized by Section 4473.

Glossary

ABSTRACT ART. Nonrepresentational design depicting no recognizable objects.

ACRYLIC PAINTS. Pigment is dispersed in acrylic emulsion. Water soluble when wet but when dry forms a permanentfilm impervious to water. Dries quickly.

ADHESIVE. Sticky substance used to connect different objects, such as glue, paste, epoxy, mucilage, etc.

ADULT. For many purposes being 18 or 21 years old signifies the start of adulthood.

ART EDUCATION. School instruction in art media, art techniques, art history, art appreciation.

ASSEMBLAGE. Three-dimensional objects joined together with other objects. May be man-made or natural forms.

AUTISM. A severely incapacitating disorder of early childhood characterized by lack of responsiveness to other people, gross deficits in language development, peculiar speech patterns.

BAREN. A Japanese instrument used to make prints by rubbing back of paper against block. Slightly convex stiff pad covered with thin bamboo.

BAT. A flat round slab of plaster used to hold clay while working.

BISQUE. Unglazed ceramic ware which has been fired. May be left in this stage or glazed.

BLINDNESS. Visual acuity of 20/200 or less in the better eye with correcting glasses; or, central acuity of more than 20/200 with the peripheral field so contracted that the widest diameter of visual field subtends an angular distance no greater than 20 degrees.

BRAIN DAMAGE. Moderate to severe injury to the brain resulting in severe behavior and/or learning disorders.

BRAYER. A small hand roller for spreading ink. May also be rubbed against back of paper to obtain finished print.

CERAMICS. Pertaining to pottery.

CEREBRAL PALSY. A condition present from birth, caused by brain damage which abnormally alters movement or functioning; may be spastic, ataxic, athetoid or mixed.

CLAY. A material found in the earth, plastic when moist, permanently hard when fired.

COLLAGE. Shaping and pasting scraps of paper, cloth and various other materials to a stiff surface. A new art used especially by Cubists and Surrealists to make a composition.

COLLAGRAPH. Intaglio process. Impression made from recessed sections of board or block on which threedimensional objects are glued. Plate is inked and surface sections are wiped clean before printing. Paper is dampened, leaving embossed surface after printing.

CRAYON. A waxlike stick impregnated with color. Usually used in schools.

CRAYPAS. A material between a crayon and a pastel (chalk).

CREATIVE SELF-EXPRESSION. The outward manifestation in an art form of what one feels internally.

CUBISM. A phase of Post-Impressionism stressing abstract forms.

DEAF. See hearing impaired.

DEVELOPMENTAL DISABILITY. According to Public Law 91-517 (42 USC 2670):

> A developmental disability is a disability attributable to mental retardation, cerebral palsy, epilepsy, or other neurological handicapping conditions of an individual, found to be closely related to mental retardation or to require treatment similar to that required by mentally retarded individuals, and the disability originates before such an individual attains age 18 and has continued, or is expected to continue indefinitely and constitutes a substantial handicap of such individuals. [Note: "autism" was added by Public Law 94-103 (29 USC 721).]

A developmemntal disability according to Public Law 95-602 (42 USC par. 6102(7)) is:

...a severe, chronic disability of a person which
(A) is attributable to a mental or physical impairment,or combination of mental and physical impairments;
(B) is manifested before the person attains age 22;
(C) is likely to continue indefinitely;
(D) results in substantial functional limitations in three or more of the following areas of life activity:
  (i)self-care
  (ii)receptive and expressive language
  (iii) learning
  (iv) mobility
  (v) self-direction
  (vi) capacity for independent living
  (vii) economic self-sufficiency; and
(E) reflects the person' s need for a combination and sequence of special, interdisciplinary, or generic care, treatment or other services which are individually planned and coordinated.

DISABILITY. A mental and/or physical limitation in functioning (see handicap).

EASEL. A stand on which to place canvas or board, usually while painting.

EMOTIONALLY DISTURBED. Characterized by one or more of the following over a long period of time and to a marked degree: inability to build or maintain satisfactory interpersonal relationships with others; inappropriate behaviors or feelings; general pervaside mood of unhappiness or depression; tendency to develop symptoms, pains or fears associated with personal problems.

ENGRAVING. Cutting into metal with a sharp tool. Used for decorative effect or as a method of making an intaglio print. Plate is inked and wiped. Print is made from ink-filled incised lines.

ENVIRONMENT. Physical, psychological and social forces, objects and people surrounding and influencing a person.

EPILEPSY. A condition in which there is loss of consciousness due to abnormal brain activity. In grand mal epilepsy loss of consciousness may be accompanied by severe convulsions; in petit mal epilepsy there is a brief loss of consciousness.

EQUIPMENT. Durable and nondurable materials and facilities which assist persons in performing their daily activities.

ETCHING. Drawing with a fine steel point or needle on a soot-blackened metal plate which has been coated with a ground of acid-resistant wax or varnish. Plate is immersed in an acid bath which bites out (etches) exposed lines. After the plate is cleaned it is inked and wiped, leaving the ink in the etched lines. Print is then made from these etched lines.

FERRULE. The metal part of the brush which holds the hair in place and attaches it to the handle.

FILLER. A substance such as powder or corn starch which is added to paint to give a certain consistency or as a cheap method for increasing the amount.

FIRING. A dry piece of pottery is placed in high heat to harden the clay and make it permanent.

Kiln. An oven which can sustain a high temperature which clay needs to become permanent.
Pit. A hole is dug in the ground and clay is fired in it at a high temperature.
Raku. A hole is dug in the ground and a glazed piece of pottery is fired at a high temperature.

FIXATIF. A varnish to adhere chalk or charcoal, usually applied by spraying.

FLAT COLOR. An area of unbroken single hue or value.

FOLK ART. Art originating with the people without the sophistication of art schools. Remains little changed throughout the generations.

GLAZING CERAMICS. A vitreous substance is applied to a clay piece and then fired, giving a glassy surface, usually in color.

GLUE. A sticky adhesive strong enough to hold various substances and objects together after drying.

GROUT. A plasterlike substance used to fill spaces between tesserae in a mosaic.

HANDICAP. Mental or physical disadvantage which renders an achievement or success more difficult (see disability).

HARD OF HEARING. See hearing impaired.

HEARING IMPAIRED. Characterized by a hearing loss ranging from mild (hard of hearing) to profound (deaf) which interferes with the development of language and speech and results in failure to achieve educational potential.

HEMIPLEGIA. Paralysis of the arm and leg on one side of the body, due to brain damage.

HUE. Applied to the names of colors, such as red, yellow, blue, etc.

INDEPENDENT LIVING. Facilities which provide partial supervision and comprehensive training directed toward the movement of individuals into self-sustaining living situations in the community. Individuals enrolled are expected to live on their own with little or no supervision.

INFERIORITY FEELING. An attitude characterized by lack of confidence, feelings of unworthiness and inadequacy.

INSTITUTIONALIZATION. Long term residence in an institution such as a state hospital for the mentally retarded or mentallly ill, prison, convalescent hospital, etc.

INTAGLIO. A print made from an engraved surface, as opposed to a planographic or relief print.

INTELLIGENCE. A person's potential for learning; may or may not reflect the influence of the environment.

INTELLIGENCE QUOTIENT (I.Q.). Score earned on an intelligence test.

INTENSITY. The degree of brilliance of a color.

JUXTAPOSITION. To place color, surfaces or objects next to each other.

KILN. A large stove or oven in which clay is fired or glazed.

LEARNING DISABILITY. Serious difficulties in learning in a person of average or above average intelligence.

MENTAL RETARDATION. Subnormal intellectual functioning associated with significant impairment in adaptive behavior with onset before age of 18 years.

MONOPRINT. Occupies a place between the graphic arts and painting. A painting done in any convenient medium which does not dry too rapidly is made on a metal or plastic plate. Paper is laid on top and rubbed, making a print. Only one impression is usually made.

MONTAGE. A picture or abstraction made by combining various ready-made elements such as drawings, paintings or photographs either whole or cut up.

MOSAIC. Surface decoration made by gluing small pieces of glass, stone, tile or other material to wood, cement or other backing.

MURAL. Large scale artistic work made on or attached to a wall.

NAIVE ART. A twentieth century individual expression of primitive quality.

NEUROLOGICAL HANDICAP. Characterized by brain damage due to prenatal, natal or postnatal disease or trauma; includes persons with Down Syndrome (mongolism), cretinism, cerebral palsy, epilepsy, and encephalopathies.

NEUROSIS. Group of mental disorders caused by unresolved internal conflicts in which no observable loss of contact with reality in thinking and judgment is present.

OIL PAINT. Pigment evenly dispersed in an oil medium or vehicle. Thinned with linseed oil or other oils. Solvent is turpentine which is flammable.

ORTHOPEDICS. The branch of medical science that deals with diagnosis and treatment of disorders involving the bones, joints and muscles.

PAPER HANGER'S OR WHEAT PASTE. A powder made from flour, wheat, rice or starch. When mixed with water, becomes a paste particularly good for paper.

PAPIER MACHE. Paper in strips or pulp fixed with paste or glue. Gets hard and strong when dry.

PARAPLEGIA. Paralysis of the lower part of the body, including both legs, due to brain or spinal cord injury.

PASTE. Preparation of flour, starch, rice, etc., prepared by adding water. Particularly good for adhering paper.

PASTEL. A colored chalk of artistic quality.

PHYSICAL DISABILITY. Characterized by serious difficulties in moving one or more parts of the body.

PLANOGRAPHIC PROCESS. To print from a flat surface, such as lithography.

PRESS. A machine which applies pressure for making a print.

PRIMITIVE ART. Emerges from a total cultural complex and has a cultural function for the whole group.

PRINTING. The act of impressing letters or pictures on paper, cloth or other material.

PSYCHOSIS. A personality disorder of sufficient severity to alienate the person from reality, with behavioral responses which are peculiar, abnormal, inefficient or definitely antisocial.

PSYCHOTHERAPY. Treatment of mental, nervous and emotional disorders by psychological methods.

QUADRIPLEGIA. Paralysis or involvement of all four extremities due to brain or spinal cord injury.

REALISTIC ART. Representation without changes. Adherence to actual fact.

RELIEF PRINT. The print is made from the surfaces of a block which have not been cut away, or it may be printed from a block whose surfaces have been built up.

ROLLER. A small hand tool that has a rubber cylinder for pressing and smoothing ink on a plate for printing. May also be used in printing.

RUBBER CEMENT. A cement consisting of a solution of unvulcanized rubber, as in solvent naphtha or carbon disulphide. Flammable, harmful vapors, not permanent.

SCHIZOPHRENIC REACTION. A psychotic disorder characterized by withdrawal from the environment, regression and deterioration of emotional response; may be episodic.

SELF-CONCEPT. Perception of and attitudes towards oneself.

SELF-ESTEEM. Feeling of worth and pride in oneself.

SELF-IMAGE. Same as self-concept.

SHADE. When black is added to a color. The darkness of a color, such as dark red, dark blue, etc.

SPASTICITY. Excessive tension of muscles causing stiff and awkward movements, due to brain.

SPEECH AND LANGUAGE IMPAIRMENT. Seriously handicapping communication disorders, impaired phonation (voice production), articulation (sound production), rhythm (stuttering and cluttering), or language dysfunctions (delayed speech, aphasia).

SYNDROME. An aggregate of symptoms which characterize a certain disease or disorder.

TACTILE. Perceptible by the touch or appealing to the touch.

TEMPERA PAINT. Pigment mixed with binder making color opaque. Soluble in water.

> *Powder Tempera.* Pigment remains in powdered stage. Must be mixed with water before use.
> *Cake Tempera.* Pigment is mixed with binder and compressed into solid cakes which dissolve when used with water.
> *Liquid Tempera.* Pigment is mixed with binder and is ready for use.

TESSERAE. Small pieces of glass, tile or stone used in a mosaic.

TEXTURE. The surface quality of painting, prints, sculpture,etc., from very smooth to very rough, e.g., texture of fur, of metal, of sandpaper, of leather, etc.

THERAPY. Any method used to treat a disease or disorder, both mental and physical.

TINT. When white is added to a color, e.g., the tint of red is pink.

TRAUMA. An injury or wound. A wound or emotional shock leaving a deep psychological impression.

TURPENTINE. A colorless liquid used as a solvent for oil paints. Flammable.

UNCONSCIOUS. That part of our personality consisting of a complex of feelings and drives of which we are unaware.

VALUE. The light and dark of a color. When white is added to a hue it is of a light value and when black is added it is of a dark value of the color.

WATER COLOR. A transparent water-based paint. Water color can be purchased in cakes or tubes.

Index